Advance Praise for *Get Pay Right*

T0332143

This is a funny, wise, and marvelously readable book about leadership and values. New to the topic? You'll see plain language analogies. Expert in the subject matter? You'll see deep historical analyses of the root causes of today's issues. Lost in the legal thicket? You'll find a clear path forward. It's required reading at my firm for everyone involved with negotiating compensation. As the authors note, "The way we allocate resources says a lot about who and what we care about."

Bob Corlett, *President and Founder of Staffing Advisors*

The authors do a great job of illustrating that pay is about a lot more than money. An organization's values show most clearly in their decisions about which work gets highly compensated—and who gets the opportunity to do which kinds of work. This is a great practical guide for business leaders who want to build high-performing organizations with fairness at the center.

Keiran Snyder, *Founder and Former CEO of Textio*

Get Pay Right

How to Achieve Pay Equity That Works

Get Pay Right

How to Achieve Pay Equity That Works

Kent Plunkett and Heather Bussing

with

Steve Boese, George LaRocque, Madeline Laurano,
Sarah Morgan, Trish Steed, and John Sumser

Society for Human Resource Management
Alexandria, Virginia | shrm.org

Society for Human Resource Management India
Mumbai, India | shrm.org/in

Society for Human Resource Management
Middle East and Africa Office
Dubai, UAE | shrm.org/mena

SHRM®
BETTER WORKPLACES
BETTER WORLD™

SHRM books and products are available from most online bookstores and through the SHRMStore at SHRMStore.org.

SHRM is a member-driven catalyst for creating better workplaces where people and businesses thrive together. As the trusted authority on all things work, SHRM is the foremost expert, researcher, advocate, and thought leader on issues and innovations impacting today's evolving workplaces. With nearly 340,000 members in 180 countries, SHRM touches the lives of more than 362 million workers and their families globally. Discover more at SHRM.org.

Library of Congress Cataloging-in-Publication Data

Names: Plunkett, Kent, author. | Bussing, Heather, author.
Title: Get pay right : how to achieve pay equity that works / Kent Plunkett and Heather Bussing.
Description: Alexandria, Virginia : Society for Human Resource Management, [2024] | Includes bibliographical references and index. | Summary: "This book is designed to help readers understand the issues about pay equity and why it is fundamental in running a business"-- Provided by publisher.
Identifiers: LCCN 2024015438 (print) | LCCN 2024015439 (ebook) | ISBN 9781586446581 (trade paperback) | ISBN 9781586446635 (pdf) | ISBN 9781586446680 (epub) | ISBN 9781586446734 (kindle edition)
Subjects: LCSH: Pay equity. | Equal pay for equal work.
Classification: LCC HD6061 .P58 2024 (print) | LCC HD6061 (ebook) | DDC 331.2/153--dc23/eng/20240430

Printed in the United States of America

PB Printing 10 9 8 7 6 5 4 3 2 1

Table of Contents

List of Figures and Tables

Figures

Tables

Foreword

Pay equity is *equal pay for comparable work that is internally equitable, externally competitive, and transparently communicated.*

Paying all employees fairly is the gateway to organizational excellence. It removes confusion and reduces friction. It unlocks productivity. It is the foundation for trust and a sense of psychological safety.

This book provides a roadmap for firms that want to create a sustainable process for achieving pay equity. The "how to" of pay equity is different from most business issues. It involves comparing things about work that are difficult to define such as effort, skills, and responsibility. Pay equity also involves comparing people, which is even harder.

When someone says, "pay equity," most people think about money. Pay is important. But pay equity is really about fairness—paying people equally based on the work they do and their performance rather than who they are or what they look like.

Treating employees fairly affects every aspect of culture. It is the heart of trust between employees and with an employer. *Paying* people fairly increases employee engagement, optimizes performance, and provides a strong return on investment. These are things that make or break a company.

I believe we can make substantial progress in narrowing the pay equity gap. We can do it faster than most predict within our organizations and across the workforce. It can be done in a generation, not the 100+ years many prognosticate.

I am an outlier in my optimism, but the logic is sound.

If just 10 percent of large US employers adopt pay equity best practices, we can close most of the gap in two decades. The reason is that larger firms will level their pay and those new pay levels will be reported. That will shift the cost of labor in recruiting markets. The other 90 percent of firms will react to the market shifts as they do today. The market price of pay will begin to reflect pay equity leveling. The 90 percent will be influenced to also pay at levels as if they did pay equity themselves.

Proving this admittedly radical hypothesis will take a few more years of study. The message is clear, however. Firms adopting pay equity best practices not only help themselves. They lead the rest of employers to the right pay practices as well. This is how we fix a challenging societal issue.

That is why this book exists.

I have spent my career thinking about the importance of compensation and pay equity in organizations. Until recently, pay equity was hard to see and measure. Most organizations ignored it unless there was a problem.

Today, there are tools that make reporting on pay equity analysis fast and easy. But they all assume that the hardest work is conducted before you use them. Reporting is relatively easy. It is just the end of the process.

The actual work of understanding workforce equity is anything but trivial. Without a total solution framework, these reporting tools can't solve the problem. That is why I set out to create an end-to-end total solution.

The goal? To help organizations think comprehensively about pay and equity with an academic framework to guide the work.

The Plunkett Pay Equity Framework is a six-step process that helps organizations find pay gaps internally while examining market data. This gives a complete picture of both internal and external factors that drive inequities. The goal of achieving pay equity involves balancing these two forces.

Internal pay equity is not enough. You must understand the impact of the external labor market. Recruiting, retention, and attrition continuously affect the pay equity balance. No pay equity analysis is complete without market data.

Solidifying the benefits of pay equity requires transparent communication. Transparency does not require publishing everyone's pay. It means managers can explain to employees how and why they are paid as they are. Employees who understand how they are paid (and why) are more engaged and work more effectively.

Confusing and obscure pay information is a primary source of workforce productivity problems. Clarity between your people and the business about the details of pay and your pay philosophy is a foundation for deeper trust. It reduces frustration, jealousy, and misunderstanding that simply slow things down.

The pundits who say that achieving pay equity in the US workforce will take centuries are wrong. But the labor market needs leadership. Relying on tools and ideas that meet minimum reporting standards is the slow way. If just 10 percent of the biggest companies followed the roadmap in this book, the competitive markets for pay would adjust accordingly and make closing wage gaps a reality in our lifetimes.

Inflation, technological change, growing global competitiveness, and changing markets will put our companies to the test. Pay equity is not just an organizational improvement project. It is the key to global competitiveness in the coming years.

—Kent Plunkett

Acknowledgments

I am blessed with the opportunity to work with dozens of talented compensation experts, practitioners, and the leading minds in the HR analyst community. We collaborated on ideas and insights at the heart of this book. Their pushback, pressure testing, and countless hours of work helped birth the Plunkett Pay Equity Framework.

Co-author Heather Bussing and Salary.com leaders Carol Ferrari, Yong Zhang, John Sumser, and Chris Fusco helped me develop the first modern comprehensive pay equity framework. I am profoundly grateful to collaborate with them.

At Salary.com, we have worked tirelessly for 25 years to expand and improve professional compensation practice. The executive team is a phenomenal brain trust whose mantra is "Get Pay Right." They take the fundamental principles of compliance and fair pay and turn them into a remarkable, best-in-class software toolset. Most software arrives void of data. Salary.com embeds essential data sets, best practices, and a disciplined taxonomy in its groundbreaking analytical tools. In my wildest dreams, I never imagined a team this good and website that over 80 million people use each year.

We listen to our 10,000+ corporate customers to learn what works, what doesn't, and where the potential for advancement exists. We work hard to simplify the complex data manipulations that ground practical pay equity implementations. Their energy and insights drive the market-leading quality of our solutions. A lot of the lessons we learned from listening to and working with our customers are at the core of this book and the Plunkett Pay Equity Framework.

This book exists because we wanted to give people a practical and useful guide to understanding pay equity, the barriers we continue to experience, how to use pay equity assessment and tools, why pay equity matters, and to provide a roadmap that companies can use to build best practices for managing and solving for pay equity.

To do that, we asked the four analysts at H3HR Advisors for their insights and research on pay equity and HR technology. They are a formidable team of individual talents who align to shape the HR Technology Industry.

Following 20 years as a practitioner and HR leader, **Trish Steed** spent the past 15 years growing her capacity to influence the evolution of HR Technology.

Steve Boese—For 30 years, Steve Boese has been the working heart of the HR Technology Industry. He spent half of that time as the chair of the HR Technology conference. He has seen it all. His sections on "Skills, Opportunities, and Equity at Work" and the "Impact of Pay Equity" clarify the relationship between the intricacies of HR and the outcomes of pay equity.

George LaRocque is the most knowledgeable person in the world on the topic of Work Technology. His ability to see how things go together is second to none. "How Technology is Changing Compensation Practices and Pay Equity" is a ticket to his ringside seat at the evolving center of the industry.

The last thank you for our H3HR team is **Karen Steed**. The impact of her work is woven throughout Chapter 8.

Sarah Morgan's discussion of pay equity as a foundation for diversity, equity, inclusion, and belonging (DEIB) is essential reading. Her various contributions to the book shine a light on the dynamic realities of a working pay equity program. Sarah is one of the foremost voices in DEIB. Her influence extends beyond her sections and into the meat of the book.

Madeline Laurano is the most disciplined analyst in the entire HR industry. Through her company Aptitude Research, she has built a 20-year practice of defining excellence in industry analysis. Her section "Pay Equity is Critical for Talent Acquisition" clarifies the impact of pay equity on the growth and maintenance of the workforce.

Thanks also to John Sumser for his analysis of the labor market, demographics, and labor shortages. He has been a most trusted advisor and friend for 25 years. Pay equity will be essential, no matter what happens with the economy.

If you don't see a writer named, my co-author, Heather Bussing, wrote it. Heather cares deeply about equity, technology, and people. Her legal and practical experience, thoughtful analysis, and sense of humor come through in every chapter. She is a brilliant collaborator and a leading voice on diversity, equity, and inclusion issues and the law.

Thanks also to Steve Browne, SHRM-SCP and chief people officer at LaRosa's Inc., and John Baldino, president of Humareso, for their real-life stories about dealing with compensation and pay equity. John and Steve are luminaries who share their time and hard-won wisdom helping both tech companies and HR address actual problems in useful and caring ways.

Last, I must thank my colleagues from Salary.com, my friends, and my family for all their support over the twenty-five years since we founded Salary.com and began this journey to start the revolution around fair and transparent pay. Thank you to my kids Dex, Christopher, and Katherine, their mother, Julianne, and of course my parents, Gregory and Linda Plunkett, who all gave part of themselves to supporting the journey and the mission. Yong Zhang has been the incredible innovator and execution engine of our company and a lifelong best friend. Kevin Plunkett, my brother, has been a deeply valuable collaborator for all these years. Andy Linn, Cathal Brown, Lan Cheng, Chris Plunkett, and Alicia Jaromin were there contributing from the beginning and are the best at what they do. I thank them along with the thousands of other teammates over the years, too many to name, who each contributed immeasurably to making transparency and fair pay a reality. I would be remiss to ignore the key financiers who believed in the vision and funded the dream including Terry Temescu, Bill Nolan, Todd Ofenloch, Strother Scott, Brad Raymond, Dean Jacobsen, and Andy Rich. Thank you for what you all have done to help Salary.com succeed and have the opportunity to help make the world a better place to live and work.

Pay equity is about more than compensation. It is about fairness, which touches every aspect of running a successful business. You are on the way to get pay equity right and reap the rewards.

Thank you for investing the time it takes to read the book. You will find it heartwarming, optimistic, and intensely practical.

—Kent Plunkett

Introduction

Pay equity is about fairness. If two people are doing the same work, they should be paid the same. But like most things having to do with fairness, it's not simple. For one thing, there's really no such thing as equal work. Two people with the same job title at the same company often do very different things and have different responsibilities.

The legal approach is to evaluate the efforts, skills, responsibilities, and working conditions and compare similar jobs to see if they are in the same general pay range.

As a practical matter, the work, people, and market continually change, making comparisons difficult, even with the best information. This is why when you mention "pay equity audit" to any HR professional, they are likely to sigh heavily, then become very busy with other extremely pressing matters.

As legislatures across the country enact new pay transparency and reporting requirements, understanding and addressing pay equity has become essential. The great news is that assessing and addressing pay equity has become much easier with the availability of data and the creation of new tools that do much of the heavy lifting.

This book is designed to help you understand the issues and why pay equity is fundamental to running your business, especially in an ongoing labor shortage. We'll also show you how to assess and address pay equity and keep things on track.

Most importantly, we hope you come away with a better understanding of the importance of fairness. Building a culture of fairness is not only a compliance issue; it's good business.

CHAPTER 1

What Is Pay Equity?

Let's start by clarifying what we're talking about, especially since we're introducing a little different take on pay equity.

Defining Modern Pay Equity

Pay equity is traditionally defined as equal pay for comparable work. While this is accurate, any effective analysis of pay equity requires consideration of what's happening both inside and outside your organization and an understanding of why people are paid what they are paid.

With that in mind, pay equity is defined as this: *equal pay for comparable work that is internally equitable, externally competitive, and transparently communicated.*

This holistic view of pay equity shifts compensation analysis from pure market pricing to a broader equity approach that is sustainable, fair, and designed for business success.

Equal Pay and Pay Equity

Pay equity and equal pay are used interchangeably and often refer to the same thing: equal pay for equal work. The trouble is that, in most legal and practical applications, there's no such thing as equal work. Even people with the exact same roles don't do the exact same thing.

Legislatures have tried to deal with this by requiring equal pay for "comparable work" or "substantially similar work." But what does that mean? And does pay have to be exactly equal? Or can it be comparable or substantially similar too? The classic legal answer is this: Well, it depends. (That's always the classic legal answer.)

Is Equal the Same?

To make sense of these concepts, we need to start with the idea that "equal" rarely means "the same" or "identical." It can, but equal usually means that there are enough similarities among different things that it's useful to group them together and treat them as basically the same.

In some cases, that can mean a lot of tolerance for differences. For example, when we talk about comparable homes in real estate, we mean structures that have the same basic size, are in similar locations, are in similar condition, and have about the same number of bedrooms and bathrooms. Basically, two comparable homes should have comparable value. Then we look at differences that may increase or decrease the general values in comparison. This is all based on what the typical buyer wants in that area, which also varies by location and individual buyer needs or wants.

Can we say that comparable houses are equal? Not really if we're talking about whether or not they're the same. Do comparable houses have equal value? Yes, give or take.

Equal Work

When we try to compare jobs, we're asking whether the work is similar enough that the roles provide the same general value to the organization. This is the place where most people think: *Hey, we already have a basic compensation hierarchy in place that tells us the value of the roles at each level.* While absolutely true, it's a backwards analysis for pay equity. Instead of looking at the actual work to see whether it should have the same pay, we would be starting with the pay to say the work is equal. For pay equity, always start by comparing the work first.

Equal Pay

Once you have looked at whether the work is comparable, then you can compare whether the people doing that work make about the same amount of money. When you look at whether two people make equal pay, that pay includes all forms of compensation, including benefits, bonuses, expense reimbursements, and basically anything the employer provides to employees. Since most organizations provide the same benefits to workers at the same level, this usually isn't an issue and you can just look at monetary compensation.

But sometimes, pay is somewhat different, especially with discretionary and performance bonuses where higher performers can end up with lower bonuses depending on who their supervisor is. Significantly different bonuses when the work, workers, and performance is the same is not equal pay.

When two workers doing similar work don't make the same general pay, there has to be a legitimate, nondiscriminatory reason for the differences. This is where you look at the individuals doing similar jobs to see if any pay differences can be justified by good business reasons. Good business reasons include different cost of living where the workers live and differences in skills, performance, or qualifications. Good business reasons do *not* include what the workers look like, whether their supervisor likes them as a friend, their religious beliefs, whom they love, their gender, their skin color, or where they came from.

Last, is the same general pay range okay or does pay have to be exactly the same? If the range is not too big, the same pay range may be considered equal, especially if there are some differences in the work. But differences seem bigger and matter more to the people who are being paid less, and the bigger the difference, the better the reasons must be to justify it.

Equity

All this brings us to the concept of equity. Equity means fair and unbiased. In law, equity refers to what is fair and just under the circumstances. Thus, pay equity means compensation that is fair and just under the circumstances. It means that people are paid fairly based on the work they do and the skills and qualifications they bring to that work. It also means that differences in pay are justified by legitimate business reasons, not discrimination and bias.

Equal pay means that two people doing comparable work make comparable pay. It doesn't have to be exactly the same, but the closer the work, the closer the pay should be. Equal pay is a comparison of compensation. Pay equity is fair pay compared to the work.

What Is Pay for Pay Equity?

When we talk about pay equity, we are comparing pay and work. Usually, we focus on whether work is comparable because pay is, well, pay. But it's a little more complicated.

The complications matter because the way you are probably assessing pay equity may not consider paid time off, the value of benefits, or other compensation like profit sharing or stock.

Basing a pay equity analysis on the pay data that runs through payroll is fine when everything else is equal. But if there are differences in the benefits you offer specific groups of employees, it's important to review.

What Is Included in Pay for Pay Equity Analysis?

For pay equity analysis, pay includes pretty much everything the employee receives from the employer. Pay is not just wages. It includes bonuses, commissions, paid leave, benefits, and reimbursements.

Under the federal Equal Pay Act (29 C.F.R. §1620.10), wages

> Include all forms of compensation irrespective of the time of payment, whether paid periodically or deferred until a later date, and whether called wages, salary, profit sharing, expense account, monthly minimum, bonus, uniform cleaning allowance, hotel accommodations, use of company car, gasoline allowance, or some other name. Fringe benefits are deemed to be remuneration for employment.

Under state laws, the definitions vary—if there is a statutory definition—but most include all forms of cash compensation, paid time off, and the value of all benefits. Some examples include the following:

- California's frequently asked questions (FAQs) on equal pay says, "Although the law does not specifically define 'wage rates,' the term refers to the wages or salary paid, and also other forms of compensation and benefits."[1]
- New York Labor Law section 190 defines wages as "the earnings of an employee for labor or services rendered, regardless of whether the amount of earnings is determined on a time, piece, commission or other basis. The term 'wages' also includes benefits or wage supplements."[2] Benefits or wage supplements include "reimbursement for expenses; health, welfare and retirement benefits; and vacation, separation or holiday pay."[3]
- Minnesota's definition of wages for equal pay is "all compensation for performance of services by an employee for an employer whether paid by the employer or another person including cash value of all compensation paid in any medium other than cash."[4]

Trying to figure out whether the value of benefits is comparable is tricky. The way insurance companies set premiums is not the same as the way regulators look at benefits from a pay equity standpoint. For example, health insurers are allowed to charge different rates based on gender and age. But these are protected classes for pay equity and discrimination laws, so you can't simply compare the premiums the employer pays for health insurance. You look at whether they have the same coverage. This is why most pay equity analysis tools stick to cash compensation.

Still, you want to evaluate all aspects of total compensation to make sure what you offer is equivalent for employees doing comparable work, including

- Benefits;
- Any tiers related to benefits;
- Bonuses;

- Retirement contributions;
- Stock and equity;
- Reimbursements;
- Equipment, phone, wellness, and other allowances; and
- Other perks.

Comparable jobs need to have comparable total compensation. If they don't, then focus on the actual work done and adjust pay and benefits if needed. Remember, you can only increase compensation to address pay equity; you can't lower pay or discontinue benefits to make pay equal for comparable work. Also, don't restructure your assessment of comparable work to fit your organization's pay or benefit scheme. That is effectively backing the jobs into existing pay rather than assessing the work to see what jobs are comparable.

When There Are Differences, Know the Reasons

The concept of equal pay does not mean exactly the same compensation in all aspects for all comparable jobs. Equal pay means the same range of pay with comparable benefits. If there are any differences, they can be justified by legitimate business factors, such as education, training, experience, or other nondiscriminatory business reasons.

There are good reasons why some people who do similar work make different amounts. And it's important to reward performance with pay. What pay equity analysis does is give you a first-level view of where pay gaps may be related to a protected factor like gender or race.

The answer is not to figure out job categories and make them perfectly equal for everyone in that category. It's to make sure you are not making compensation decisions that end up adversely affecting certain groups. In order to do that, you need to consider everything that goes into compensation. When there are differences in pay or benefits between people doing comparable work, keep records on the business reasons for the differences.

Before you have to explain why people are paid differently, make sure you know why and that the reasons relate to experience, qualifications, and objective assessments of performance. If you can't tell a story that makes good business sense, then it's probably better to address the pay gap.

Five Differences between Direct and Indirect Compensation

- **Form**: Direct compensation is monetary and comes in the form of wages, salaries, commissions, and bonuses. Indirect compensation is nonmonetary and comes in the form of benefits such as health insurance, retirement plans, vacation and sick leave, and so on.
- **Visibility**: Direct compensation is more visible and tangible to the employee since it's included in the paycheck. Indirect compensation, however, might not be immediately noticeable to an employee as it includes often "invisible" benefits.
- **Taxation**: Direct compensation is usually taxable, with some exceptions like certain types of bonuses or commissions. Indirect compensation, on the other hand, often offers tax advantages for both the employer and employee.
- **Flexibility**: Direct compensation is often fixed based on the contract or hourly rate and can be increased based on performance or promotion. Indirect compensation can be more flexible, and companies can offer a wide variety of benefits to attract and retain employees.
- **Long-Term Value**: While direct compensation provides immediate financial gain, indirect compensation often carries long-term value and security, such as retirement plans and health insurance.

Common Barriers to Pay Equity

You would think that the biggest barrier to pay equity is pay—money. But most organizations don't even know they have pay equity issues. Money hasn't even come into the picture yet. Instead, the biggest barrier to pay equity is not knowing you have a problem. You look around and see people representing lots of colors, genders, and ages. It looks good. Everything must be fine.

Except we are humans making employment decisions about other humans. We do the best we can. And sometimes it's not good enough. Sometimes, we have to look a little deeper to see what's actually happening. This is the entire premise behind people analytics. Pay equity is another analytic you should review regularly.

When you do the pay equity audit and review the results, it's likely you will find pay gaps. Most pay equity audits also will tell you how much it will cost to close those gaps. That's when budget and money become a barrier to pay equity.

Closing pay gaps is pretty straightforward. You start with the biggest problem, figure out how much money you have, and make a plan to fix it. Even if you can't do it all right away, begin where you are. But the other big barriers to pay equity are harder both to see and to fix.

Lack of Salary Structure

When negotiating compensation is completely market driven and every open role is negotiated separately each time, it's easy for pay equity issues to arise.

Salary structures for comparable jobs help keep compensation in line, or at least boxes. Better yet, when you're figuring out which jobs belong at which pay levels, consider whether the compensation and benefits are keeping you competitive and incenting the performance and outcomes you're looking for.

In other words, do you understand why people make the pay they make, and does the way you pay people support the performance you want? Looking at pay equity can reveal other areas where change would benefit the organization.

Wage Compression

A good salary structure will have enough room at each level to find and hire the people you need, allowing for a range of experience and pay. This isn't always true, but it follows the common model of people starting something new, gaining skills, and progressing in both pay and responsibility.

When wages are increasing, it's common to hire new people at the same or even higher salary than your existing employees with more tenure. This makes the wage range smaller (the compression part).

When more people are needed quickly and hired at higher wages, senior people may end up making less than new people. This causes senior people to think about leaving for better pay, and you will have to replace them at an even higher salary.

It also can create pay equity issues depending on the demographics of your workforce and who is coming in. If your diversity, equity, and inclusion (DEI) initiatives have been successful and you've created a fairly diverse workforce, but then you hire more White guys for more money because you need people fast, you will end up with pay gaps based on race and gender. It's the market. You didn't intend for it to be this way. But it's still a problem, both legal and practical.

Bias

On one end, bias is simply a preference for one thing over another. Would you rather have a chocolate or lemon cupcake? Vanilla with sprinkles? On the other end, bias is illegal discrimination where our preferences result in making employment decisions that adversely affect people because of their race, religion, gender, or other protected factors.

Because most people making employment decisions continue to be White and people tend to favor people more like them, we end up with discrimination far more often than we think. It's usually not conscious or intentional.

This results in pay equity issues because women and minorities make less than White men for substantially similar work. Women experience pay gaps in all occupations no matter their education or qualifications.

Pay equity is about compensating people fairly for their work, regardless of who the person is doing the work. Next we'll delve deeper into the history of gender and racial wage gaps, what's different now, and how to use pay equity as a foundation for fairness in compensation and throughout your organization.

CHAPTER 2

The Problem of Unfair Pay and Why It Matters

When we start to ask, "What problem are we trying to solve?" it quickly becomes clear that it's not just pay. Pay gaps and inequities are a symptom of a larger issue, which is bias and, in some cases, discrimination.

Pay Equity Is About More Than Money

Pay equity is only partly about pay. And a lot of what *is* about pay is also about other essential aspects of running an organization. Compensation is the heart of a company's relationship with its employees. As a result, it has an impact on every area of the HR department. Here are some of the key places where compensation can affect what happens.

> **Recruitment and Talent Acquisition**: Compensation can impact an organization's ability to attract and retain top talent. If compensation is not competitive or equitable, it may be challenging to attract and retain qualified candidates. Therefore, compensation plays a vital role in recruitment and talent acquisition.
>
> **Job Analysis and Job Design**: The compensation package is based on the job's duties, responsibilities, and requirements. Therefore, compensation can influence job analysis and job design.

Performance Management: Performance management involves setting performance goals, providing feedback, and evaluating performance against those goals. Compensation can be tied to performance, so it can play a significant role in performance management.

Employee Engagement and Retention: Employees who feel fairly compensated for their work are more likely to be engaged and committed to their job and the organization. Therefore, compensation can play a crucial role in employee engagement and retention.

Compliance Management: Compensation is subject to several legal and regulatory requirements, such as minimum wage laws, overtime regulations, and anti-discrimination laws. Therefore, compensation can impact compliance management.

Benefits Administration: The value and cost of employee benefits are often tied to the compensation package. Therefore, compensation can have an impact on benefits administration.

Succession Planning: Compensation can impact succession planning by providing incentives and career development opportunities for employees who have the potential to take on leadership roles in the organization.

Training and Development: Compensation can impact an organization's ability to provide training and development opportunities for employees. If compensation is not competitive, the organization may not have the resources to invest in employee development.

Workforce Planning: Compensation can impact workforce planning by influencing the organization's ability to attract and retain talent, as well as by providing incentives for employees to stay with the organization.

Diversity, Equity, and Inclusion: Compensation can impact diversity, equity, and inclusion (DEI) efforts by ensuring that all employees are fairly compensated regardless of their gender, race, ethnicity, or other characteristics. Additionally, compensation can be used to promote DEI by providing incentives for employees to participate in DEI initiatives.

Employee Relations: Compensation can impact employee relations by influencing employee morale and satisfaction. If employees feel that they are not fairly compensated, it can lead to low morale and dissatisfaction.

Organizational Development: Compensation can impact organizational development by influencing the culture of the organization. If the compensation structure is not equitable, it can create a culture of distrust and disengagement.

HR Analytics: Compensation data can be used to generate insights and analytics that can help inform HR decisions related to talent management, workforce planning, and organizational development.

This is why getting compensation, and especially pay equity, right can make a difference for your entire organization.

Inequities in Pay Often Reflect Bias

Sometimes pay inequities just happen. The most common situation is that newer people get hired in a tight labor market at a higher rate than existing employees who have been there longer and have more experience and responsibilities. Often, though, pay gaps are the result of historical and cultural barriers for women and people of color, who have always and continue to make less money than men, especially White and Asian men.

This is not any particular person, group, or organization's fault. Determining fault is not useful here. Long-held ideas about the roles of men and women in work and families; historical prejudice against Black, Latinx, and Indigenous people; and the tendency of people in power to choose people like themselves have all contributed to universal gender and racial pay gaps in every profession.

To give you a sense of how pervasive pay inequities are, we'll explain the current reality of how compensation still depends on who you are and what you look like.

The Gender Pay Gap

The gender pay gap is the difference between what men and women make for the same work. In the US, women still earn about 83 cents for each dollar men make. But it's not just earnings. The American Association of University Women have determined that as of 2020, women have only 32 percent of the wealth that men have, have only 70 percent of the retirement funds (for those who have any), and also carry two-thirds of the nation's student debt.[1]

In mid-2022, Harvard Business Review published a study[2] of Massachusetts Bay Transportation Authority train operators. The workers are all union members and pay is negotiated by contract, removing most of the opportunities for gender bias. Nonetheless, women train operators made 89 cents for every dollar men made. The reason? Shifting schedules that made it hard for women to handle all the responsibilities they have outside of work, such as caring for children and taking elderly parents to doctor appointments. In particular, the opportunities for overtime shifts were unpredictable and available on short notice. Because women had additional (unpaid) obligations, they could not work the overtime shifts.

In late 2022, McKinsey released their Women in the Workplace report that explored women in leadership in 333 organizations that employ more than 12 million people. Women are still underrepresented in leadership, and the barriers for advancement continue: their judgment is questioned, they are mistaken for someone more junior, and they continue to have significant burdens outside of work:

> For every 100 men who are promoted from entry level to manager, only 87 women are promoted, and only 82 women of color

are promoted. As a result, men significantly outnumber women at the manager level, and women can never catch up.[3]

Women leaders are also leaving companies at an extraordinary rate: "For every woman at the director level who gets promoted to the next level, two women directors are choosing to leave their company."[4] This affects both organizations and the gender pay gap. When women, particularly women of color, cannot advance to higher-paying leadership roles, the pay gap will continue.

History of the Gender Pay Gap

Historically, the concept of the man as "breadwinner" comes from nineteenth-century England, where economists asserted there was a necessary gender division where men were "producers" and women were dependent on men to support them.[5] This meant that men's work was more important and more highly valued than women's work. Men needed to make more to support their families. If women worked, they were taking jobs from men who needed them. Even when women entered the workforce during World War I because the men were fighting (and the work still had to be done), the women were later forced to quit their jobs so men returning from the war could have them.

Many women could not own property until the mid-1800s.[6] Women could not vote in US elections until 1920.[7] Even then, it was only White women. It wasn't until the women's movement of the 1970s that women got some power to control their own finances and lives. Women could not get a credit card in their own name until 1974, could not serve on a jury in some states until 1975, and did not have protections against getting fired because they were pregnant until 1978.[8] Sexual harassment did not become illegal until 1980, when it was recognized as a form of gender discrimination by the Equal Employment Opportunity Commission. The Supreme Court first recognized sexual harassment as a form of workplace discrimination in 1986.[9] While women have had legal rights and protections for more than fifty years, there still is a significant gender pay gap.

Current Drivers of the Gender Pay Gap

That women give birth and still do the majority of child rearing and household work continues to be a primary driver of income inequality between men and women.[10] Cultural assumptions that men should be paid more because they have families to support are still common. The reality is that in 40 percent of US households, women are the primary or sole earner.[11]

Cultural biases about what kinds of jobs women should do persist, even though women make great construction workers, firefighters, engineers, and especially chief executive officers (CEOs).[12] Occupations that historically have been held by women, such as teaching, social work, and nursing, are often lower-paying jobs. But in those occupations, men still make more.[13] Even in jobs like accounting, where women make up more than 58 percent of the profession, women are paid 80 cents for each dollar men earn.

Racial Pay Gaps Compound Pay Inequities

There is also a significant racial wage gap that affects both men and women. This means that women of color get penalized twice. The racial breakdown of average women's earnings compared to men of the *same* race is as follows:[14]

- Asian: 71 percent,
- White: 83 percent,
- Black: 90 percent, and
- Latina: 86 percent.

In the past two decades, the Black–White wage gap has increased for workers of all education levels. Economist Elise Gould found that the average overall Black–White pay gap increased from 21.8 percent in 2000 to 26.5 percent in 2019.[15] The gaps widened with every level of education: from 15.3 percent to 18.3 percent for high school, 17.2 percent to 22.5 percent for college, and 12.5 percent to 17.6 percent for advanced degree holders. This indicates that education alone is not the problem.

In 2019, Black advanced degree holders earned on average 82.4 cents to the dollar of White advanced degree holders. Even a multiple regression analysis that controlled for education level, age, sex, and geographic region revealed a worsening pay gap for Black workers, from 10.2 percent in 2000 to 14.9 percent in 2019.[16]

In the case of Asian workers, on average Asian men make more than White men, although the pay gap between Asian men and Asian women is almost 30 percent. Latinx and Indigenous workers make the least (see Figure 2.1).

The wage gap is not closing any time soon. If we continue to make progress at the current rate, Black women will not see pay equity until 2369, and Latinas will have to wait almost one hundred years longer—until 2451.

Why Efforts to Address the Problem Haven't Worked

While laws mandating equal pay have been around for sixty years, not much has changed. The reason is that the laws have generally addressed pay rather than the systemic biases at work.

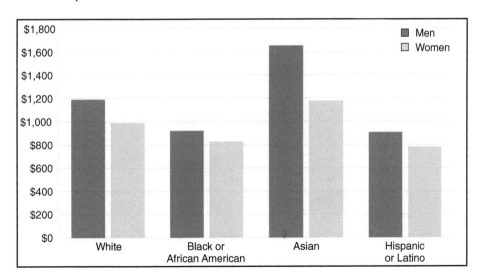

Figure 2.1. Gender Pay Gap by Race: Median Usual Weekly Earnings of Full-Time Wage and Salary Workers by Race, Hispanic or Latino Ethnicity, and Gender—3rd Quarter 2022, Not Seasonally Adjusted (*Source*: Bureau of Labor Statistics)

The Equal Pay Act

As part of the civil rights movement, the Equal Pay Act was passed by Congress in 1963, making it illegal to pay men and women differently for the same work. The problem is that generally men and women do different work. In 2018, the *New York Times* published a list of jobs where men of one first name outnumbered all the women in the same role.[17] For example, in Fortune 500 companies, there are more CEOs named John than women CEOs.

Women make up the majority of workers in the lowest-paying professions. Of the twenty lowest-paying professions, women are the majority in fifteen (mostly domestic workers). Of the twenty highest-paying jobs, women are the majority in four (pharmacists, nurse practitioners, physician assistants, and veterinarians). The 2021 data from the Bureau of Labor Statistics (BLS; see Figures 2.2–2.5) show that not much has changed with pay equity (even though a lot has changed in the world).

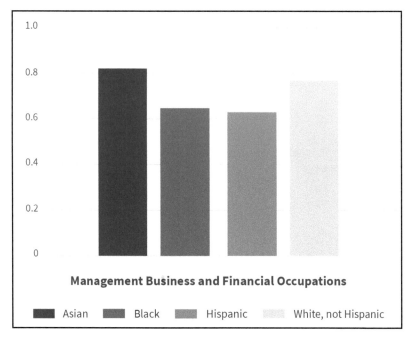

Figure 2.2. What Women Make Compared to White Men: Management Business and Financial Occupations (*Source*: US Census Data)

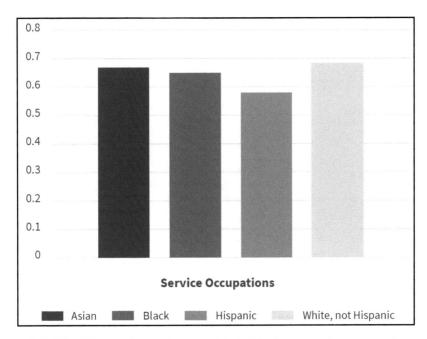

Figure 2.3. What Women Make Compared to White Men: Service Occupations (*Source*: US Census Data)

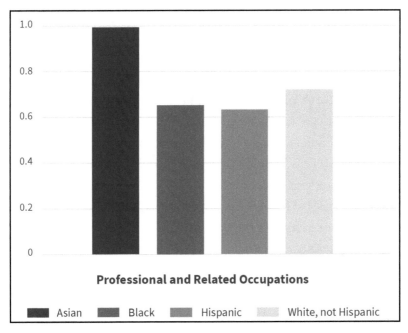

Figure 2.4. What Women Make Compared to White Men: Professional and Related Occupations (*Source*: US Census Data)

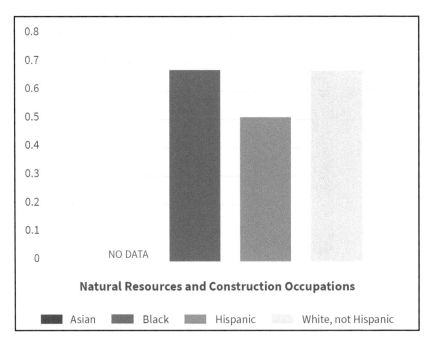

Figure 2.5. What Women Make Compared to White Men: Natural Resources and Construction Occupations (*Source*: US Census Data)

For example:

- Women teachers in the US outnumber men roughly three to one.
- Women nurses outnumber men by nearly eight to one, according to the Institute for Women's Policy Research.
- Half of physicians are women, but they are overly represented in pediatrics and obstetrics and gynecology, which are among the lower-paying specialties.
- Women are less than a third of workers in science and engineering.
- Black women earned 24 percent of doctorates in science, technology, engineering, and math (STEM), but only 5 percent of managerial jobs in STEM were held by Black women and men combined.

There are *only five jobs* where women usually make more than men. Only pharmacists are in the top-paying professions:

- Compliance officers,
- Graphic designers,
- Clinical laboratory technologists and technicians,
- Pharmacists, and
- Insurance claims and policy processing clerks.

The professions with the largest pay gaps are presented in Table 2.1.

Although gender pay equity has been federal law since 1963, even the lawyers are still paying women 60 cents for every dollar men make.

So the Equal Pay Act has not done much to change pay equity simply because it failed to address the fact that men and women still do different work. And even though women and people of color have made inroads to higher-paying jobs, they are still paid less.

Salary Ban and Pay Transparency Laws

Between 2017 and 2023, thirty states (including Washington, DC and Puerto Rico) and some cities banned asking job candidates about their current or past salary or prohibited discriminating against someone because they declined to disclose past compensation.

These laws address the fact that when someone discloses their past pay, the current employer usually negotiates from there rather than what the employer pays others or the market value for the similar roles. By requiring employers to independently value the job, candidates get a fresh start, free of past pay discrimination.

Table 2.1. Professions with Largest Gender Pay Gaps

Rank	Occupation	Percent less that females earn compared to males
1	Securities, commodities, and financial services sales agents	44
2	Legal occupations	40
3	Medical scientists	40
4	Personal financial advisors	35
5	Engineering technologists and technicians	34

Source: Business.org

Between 2018 and 2023, seven states and a handful of cities (mostly in NY, NJ, and OH) passed laws requiring employers to disclose the salary range for the role to candidates and current employees upon request. California, Colorado, Washington, and New York City all require that the pay range be posted in the job ad.

The purpose of pay transparency laws is to require employers to determine the range for the role before the hiring process so that it is not tied to a specific candidate. In places where the salary range must be disclosed in the job posting, it makes that information public, which, in turn, makes the market more transparent.

When everyone is negotiating based on the same information, it creates a fairer process. It also saves everyone time because it avoids the common situation where a candidate gets an offer but won't accept because the pay doesn't work.

Gary Straker, Vice President of Compensation Consulting at Salary.com, has received questions about how broad or narrow the pay ranges should be as employers grapple with disclosing information they have considered confidential. "The key to determining the pay range to post is whether it is realistic," Straker said. "Does the employer have people making salaries in the range, and does the range reflect what the employer is willing to pay?"

Can Laws Solve Pay Equity?

Pay equity laws are a great start. Making pay more transparent is also fundamental to equalizing knowledge between employers and employees. But the key to equality is making equal opportunity real. That means placing women and people of color in leadership roles and shifting power structures to be more inclusive and diverse. Sarah Morgan, director of equity and inclusion at Humareso, has a great discussion in Chapter 3 on how we can use pay equity as the foundation for DEI.

Yet laws alone usually don't work to change social issues. The trouble is that most laws are designed to punish infractions after they have happened. They only look backwards after the harm is done. And lawsuits are expensive, time-consuming, and cannot begin to address every violation.

Some newer laws on pay transparency include a safe harbor provision that suspends all liability for a period of 2–3 years to allow organizations to bring their practices, processes, and pay equity into compliance. This approach rewards organizations for regularly assessing pay equity and gives them the opportunity to address any issues without penalty. Approaches like this that encourage organizations to look at and fix pay equity within realistic time frames (often shorter than lawsuits) are encouraging because they are focused on improving pay equity going forward instead of penalizing past problems.

What Pay Equity Can't Solve

Pay equity is just the start is reducing bias; it doesn't directly address the bigger problem of helping people grow and succeed in an organization. That's because pay equity only works with jobs that are comparable, to assess whether the pay is also comparable. It doesn't look at whether people get promoted equally and have the same opportunities for development and growth within the organization.

A diversity audit can help assess what's happening overall and is another aspect of compliance and equity since that information is also required for EEO-1 reporting. California is also requiring more detailed reporting on both diversity and pay.

Pay equity is a great place to start, though. It focuses on the work and pay before anyone looks at who is doing that work. And, unlike unconscious bias, pay is relatively straightforward to deal with.

But don't forget to track what happens next to look at whether the organization is also fairly distributing opportunity.

Budget as a Statement of Values

The way we allocate resources says a lot about whom and what we care about. That we are still not making much progress, and in some cases sliding backwards, on pay equity means that we still don't have our priorities straight. Yet money matters to everyone. Money can be a great place to start changing how things are. It's much easier to change our budget than to eliminate hundreds of years of historical and cultural bias. By walking the talk and putting money where our aspirations lie, we can make pay equity the foundation for change.

CHAPTER 3

Pay Equity as the Foundation of Diversity, Equity, and Inclusion

by Sarah Morgan

Pay equity and compensation transparency are the cornerstones of a comprehensive diversity, equity, and inclusion (DEI) strategy. Without a commitment to paying employees fairly and taking consistent action to ensure this happens, efforts to increase the diversity demographics of employees and steps taken to ensure all employees feel welcomed and accepted ultimately ring hollow and performative. By not committing tangibly to pay equity, an organization demonstrates that it lacks true commitment to the well-being, stability, and growth of its employees.

DEI leaders must cultivate and maintain keen awareness in themselves that pay equity is a cornerstone of effective compensation strategy. They also must understand how power dynamics and the intersecting identities of people play significant roles in how wages are determined, set, and corrected. It is typically not difficult for most DEI leaders to understand and appreciate these facts. The difficulty comes in convincing organizational leadership of this and moving leadership toward action to eradicate the problem— first within the organization and then within their sphere of greater societal influence.

Get Support and Resources

If the organization is new in its commitment to DEI or if the DEI leader is new to the organization, convincing leadership will begin with assessing the organization's awareness of the systemic drivers of pay equity as well as its understanding of how power and privilege perpetuate the cycle. If awareness within the organization is low, the DEI leader will have a difficult, if not impossible, task ahead of them in getting the organization to take action to overcome pay equity issues. If the leadership of the organization believes that equal pay for equal work is not possible because of the intersecting variables that typically accelerate the pay of some individuals over others, then leadership is committed to the existing power dynamic structures.

Convincing leadership that redistributing power is the better approach to handling pay will be a Sisyphean undertaking where progress will likely be slow and arduous. The DEI leadership will have to guide the organizational leadership through unlearning the longstanding existing power dynamics, understanding and embracing the role of intersecting identities on pay decisions, and learning a new approach where equity is centered and all decisions about pay are made with intentionality toward maintaining fairness and transparency. Again, this is a very difficult shift for organizational leadership to make when it has little to no existing awareness. The DEI leader in this circumstance will have a long road ahead of them, not just with pay equity but likely with all DEI programming efforts.

If the organizational leadership has a moderate to high level of awareness, and a willingness to commit to learning a new approach, the next step for the DEI leader is to begin the pay equity audit described later in this book. While the pay equity audit is being conducted, the DEI leader should begin work with financial decision-makers in the organization on the resources that may be needed to implement corrections.

Depending on the organization's existing compensation philosophy and practices, the money needed to correct disparities the first time an organization completes a pay equity audit can be considerable. The DEI leader should not let this be a surprise for those responsible for financial decisions. Instead, they should start working with financial decision-makers as early as possible in the process to determine how the organization is going to correct the pay gaps the audit is likely to find.

Communicate about DEI and Pay Equity

Another important step in the process of establishing the organization's commitment to DEI and to pay equity is communication. Because there is more to DEI than just pay equity, it is essential for the organization to communicate its commitment to DEI and regularly share the actions it is taking or will take to advance the goals associated with this commitment. Table 3.1 presents a few examples of DEI events and actions that an organization should share formal communications about.

Because there are so many ways this commitment can manifest, the examples for this would be too exhaustive to list. Table 3.1 gives a general overview for a few key areas covered for organizations beginning the DEI commitment journey. As a best practice, during the first 18–24 months of committing to DEI, the organization should include a communication element directly for those impacted by the action and a general communication for the organization at large. The organization may also want to consider a

Table 3.1. Chart of DEI Actions That Require Formal Communications

Event or action	Individual	Organization-wide	Public
Decision to commit to DEI as an organization	√	√	√
Pay equity audit	√	√	
Compensation strategy and structure changes	√	√	√*
Hiring and promotion practice changes	√	√	
DEI educational programming	√	√	√
Affinity and resource group establishment and events	√	√	
Identity, inclusion, and engagement survey and results	√	√	
DEI programming roadmap	√	√	√*

*Denotes this is optional, situational, or required

public communication to share on its website and social media channels as well, depending on the significance of the event and its disclosure requirements. The DEI leader should be involved with crafting and editing these messages to ensure appropriate language and centering in the communication. Without this input, the impact of communications can be diminished because of unintentional errors, or the communications can come across as performative and insincere.

Organizations cannot proclaim to be committed to DEI and stand still on the issue of pay equity. Failing to take action to achieve pay equity is essentially saying the organization is okay with the current status quo that pays certain individuals more than others for the same or substantially similar work because those individuals belong to certain identity groups. This is the organization essentially saying that it values certain identity groups more than others. This is ethically, morally, and legally unacceptable. For this reason, organizations must take a stand and take appropriate action to eliminate the wage gap and achieve pay equity within its ranks.

The way for organizations to commit to this is by raising awareness and understanding of how systemic capitalism, sexism, and racism create power dynamics in the organization that perpetuate warped thinking about which people are deserving of opportunities and access and which people are not. Once the organization understands this, it must begin to redefine and redistribute access, opportunity, power, and resources more equitably.

How Power Dynamics Perpetuate Inequities

Before diving into the commonly identified reasons for these gaps, it is important to understand the power dynamics and identity groups involved as well as how this plays out in business and the workplace. Power is defined as the amount of authority and influence an individual holds over another individual or group. Power dynamics is the balance of controlling behaviors exerted between an individual or group and another individual or group. When someone with power uses it to exercise intense and severe control over another, the power is said to be imbalanced. The same is true when someone with power uses none of it. The ideal is to keep power balance such that the individual or group with less power is still given ample choice and is treated with respect, fairness, and dignity throughout interactions with the individual or group with more power.

What capitalism alongside sexism and racism has done to our world over the last five hundred years is (a) use our visible and known differences to deem certain individuals as more deserving of power than others, (b) convince us that access to power can and should only be earned through narrowly defined identities, and (c) normalize the notion that sharing power and the resources that accompany it should be avoided at all costs because it will lead to societal collapse where everyone loses both power and resources. Because of this, those who gain power are generally committed to keeping it and are willing to wield it harshly over others to maintain it.

Table 3.2 provides an overview of the groups that people are commonly divided into based on their belonging to certain identities by birth, choice, or other circumstance.

Those in the power majority groups, while being the smallest segment of the worldwide population, generally have more authority and influence in business and workplaces than the other two groups. Those in the middle group have limited access to authority and influence based on their adherence to the norms set by the power majority. However, the power of the middle group can and will be removed by the power majority if the middle group uses too much of the power granted to them to provide aid, encouragement, and support to those in the restricted power access group. Meanwhile, the group with restricted power access are among the largest segments of the worldwide population but have the least amount of power.

It is also important to remember that our identities are intersecting. Within one person can exist a power majority, limited power access, and restricted power access identity at the same time. Within another, only power majority identities, limited power access, or restricted power access identities may exist. Depending on the intersections of identities, this may cause some individuals to struggle with yielding to authority, and they may try to exert influence in opposition to power majority norms while operating in a limited or restricted power access position.

Table 3.2. Chart of Groups by Power Held in Organization

Power Majority	Limited Power Access	Restricted Power Access
People holding executive and revenue-generating jobs	People holding operational, people management, and financial management jobs	People holding staff and administrative jobs
White collar workers	Grey collar and frontline workers	Blue collar and essential workers
People educated at 4-year college or beyond	People educated at a 2-year, community college, specialized school, or other continuing education institution	People who graduated from high school, and people with a General Educational Development certificate (GED) or less than high school
Physically and mentally neurotypical people	Physically or mentally disabled and/or neurodiverse people with invisible and/or less acute conditions	Visibly and/or acutely physically or mentally disabled and/or neurodiverse people
Rich or wealthy people	People earning a living wage	People earning low wages and/or living at, just above, or below the poverty line
White people	Assimilated, White-presenting, and White-passing Black, Indigenous, Latinx, Asian, and Middle Eastern Indian people	Non-assimilated, non-White presenting, and non-White passing Black, Indigenous, Latinx, Asian, and Middle Eastern Indian people
Cisgender heterosexual men	Feminine-presenting cisgender women, cisgender people with same gender attraction and relationships	Masculine-presenting or non-binary cisgender women, feminine-presenting or non-binary cisgender men, feminine-presenting gay men, masculine-presenting lesbian women, queer people, bisexual or pansexual or asexual people, people who question their gender identity and sexual attraction, transgender people
Cisgender heterosexual married men with biological children	Cisgender heterosexual married women with biological children	All other people with children, biological or non-biological
Cisgender heterosexual men who are caregivers	Cisgender heterosexual women who are caregivers	All other people who are caregivers
European ethnicities	Asian and Middle Eastern Indian ethnicities	African, Latin, and Indigenous ethnicities
Christian religions	Jewish, Hindu, and Buddhist religions	Islamic religions, Indigenous, African, and Latin spiritual practices, and non-religious or atheist practices

Since those in the power majority groups are the ones typically in charge of business and making decisions about policy and practice in workplaces, they are the ones setting the pay wages for themselves and for the other groups. Because of the capitalism, sexism, and racism embedded into our industrialized societal norms, the power majority is setting pay as higher for those who share power majority identity with them and setting pay as lower for those in the limited and restricted power access groups. The wages are set this way because power majority logic tells those in the power majority that their value to the world is greater and, by extension, that the work they perform in business and workplaces is more significant than that of those in the middle and traditionally marginalized groups; therefore, those in the power majority believe that they deserve more pay. This is then reinforced by the power majority groups repeatedly through the laws, policies, and practices they enact and enforce, which in turn keeps those power majority groups in power even as new individuals enter the world and the workforce. This is the underlying driver of the ongoing systemic issues of our societies that keep pay equity a perennial issue to overcome for those with limited and restricted power identities.

The effect of capitalism, sexism, and racism on our power dynamics in society and workplaces has had serious and lasting negative impacts on the power majority, limited power access, and restricted power groups. Here are some of the most common impacts:

> **Financial:** The people from limited power access and restricted power access identities who are paid less than those with power majority identities for the same or substantially similar work will earn at least $10,000 less per calendar year. Most people will work full-time for 40–50 years before retiring either partially or fully. This means pay inequity will result in individuals with limited power access and restricted power access identities earning almost $500,000 less in their working lifetime than those with power majority identities.
>
> The lost earnings of those with limited power access and restricted power access identities over the course of their working

lifetime results in them having less disposable income. This leaves them less able to fully participate in the cycle of our economy. They are unable to save and invest as much, so they retire with less money. They are also unable to spend as much, so their local and state economies do not thrive at the same levels as those in the power majority.

The lack of disposable income also reduces the ability of those with limited power access and restricted power access identities to take full advantage of services relating to their health and welfare because they cannot afford it. This worsens how people with limited power access and restricted power access identities are impacted by chronic and catastrophic illness as well as their longevity of life and their mortality rates.

Psychological: Knowing that you are being paid less than your coworker for the same or substantially similar work is a demoralizing experience. As this practice continues throughout a person's career, it can lead to a sense of hopelessness and repressed anger, which impacts a person's ability to deliver consistently on work outputs. This is an underlying driver in "quiet quitting," an existing issue that has been highlighted and discussed often. Quiet quitting is the idea that people are not going above and beyond at work anymore, choosing to just meet their specific job description and requirements only. This is also an underlying driver in low employee engagement. Employee engagement is the strength of the mental and emotional connection employees feel toward the work they do. Those with traditionally marginalized identities are more likely to be disengaged and quietly quit because they do not believe the organization respects or cares for them because it is not paying them fairly or equitably.

Meanwhile, those with power majority identities develop a false sense of confidence in their superiority. When their identity or false superiority are challenged, they become defensive and retaliatory toward individuals in the limited power access and restricted power access groups who challenge or offend them. This false confidence and defensiveness is an underlying driver in why pay equity challenges are so difficult to overcome and eradicate. Those with power majority identities have had authority and influence for so long and the idea that their identity is superior is perpetuated so widely that they are unable to see any other options as being factual or true. This leaves them unable to see ways that shared or reduced power and redistribution of resources to those in the limited power access and restricted power access groups can be effective in the short or long term. Some with power majority identities do not even believe those in the limited power access and restricted power access identity groups are even worthy of such consideration. This mentality is dangerous to workplaces and the progress needed to eliminate the wage gap.

Pay Equity Is a Great Place to Start Because Now, It's Easy to See

Unlike many other areas of DEI strategy, pay equity is easily determined and can be easily corrected when discrepancies are discovered. Pay equity is ultimately a math problem with a clear financial solution. Either the 2+2 for Employee A equals the 2+2 for Employee B or it doesn't. When an organization discovers that the pay for one employee does not match the pay for another in a comparable position, the organization should also discover a reason attributable to some combination of organizational tenure, documented performance, related education, or prior workplace experience. If no such reason is found, a pay inequity exists that must be corrected. Any other approach is akin to the organization publicly admitting that it does not care about fairness or about closing the wage gap that has been proven to cause significant harm to people of traditionally marginalized identities, their families, and communities. There is no legitimate DEI strategy without a focused, intentional approach to pay equity.

CHAPTER 4

Compensation Philosophy and Strategy

Considering pay equity is an ideal time to look at your overall compensation philosophy and strategy. Is there a coherent set of values and criteria to explain why people make the compensation they make? If it's complicated or messy, that's absolutely normal. But it's worth the time and effort to step back and review the organization's approach to compensation and articulate what you're trying to do with pay and assess if it's working.

Pay Equity as Part of a Larger Compensation Strategy

A compensation strategy sets out the organization's approach to pay and benefits. It establishes the guiding principles on compensation decisions and looks at pay in the context of the organization's overall goals. Your compensation strategy should be consistent with the organization's business strategy, the performance the organization wants to encourage, and, of course, the budget.

Creating a compensation strategy means thinking about how to meet the fundamental needs of the organization and the people who work there. It's considering what the company wants to achieve in a certain timeframe, what it needs to get there, and how to find the resources and workers who can do it. The difficulty is that every organization's goals and needs are going to be different. It's a custom-fit process that requires consideration of the work, the market, and predictions about what may happen. There are many ways to do it right, and you and your organization's leaders are the experts on what will work for you.

Why All Organizations Need A Compensation Strategy

Labor costs are the biggest line item of most organizations' budget.[1] And having the right people doing the work is what makes a business successful. Therefore, getting pay right is essential to operations, no matter what your industry or company size. Having a clear compensation strategy will also help you recruit and retain employees and make budgeting and planning easier and more straightforward.

Recruiting

Even if you are not planning on hiring soon, you may have people leave (or want someone to leave). When you are hiring for an unexpected opening, you want to understand whom you need, where to find them, and what the going pay for the role is. For larger organizations who can predict their overall turnover, although not usually who will leave, having guiding principles for salary ranges, incentive pay, benefits, and other pay decisions makes negotiations smoother and faster for everyone.

Retention

Pay raises are usually larger when people change than if they stay for the annual cost-of-living adjustment and scheduled pay increase. While changing jobs involves many factors besides pay, being prepared to meet the market can be a key to keeping the people you have.

Budget and Planning

It's much better to be able to plan for raises and handle budgeting for benefits when you know your strategy for compensation in general, know what's going on in the market, and have thought through your approach to staying competitive. Some organizations take a straightforward approach and address base pay. Others may not have budget for big raises but can compete with other benefits, flexible schedules, or remote work. The important thing is to have the information you need, know your priorities, and have the guiding principles in place.

Pay Equity

Pay equity is an essential piece of compensation strategy. This is where the commitment to diversity, equity, and inclusion (DEI) and pay equity become real by committing to and budgeting to close pay gaps. As new people are hired at higher rates, it's essential to track what's happening overall with pay equity and whether any pay gaps can be justified for legitimate business reasons or whether there is potential bias that can be correlated to gender, race, age, or other protected factors. Most pay equity issues are not intentional and can be difficult to spot. Monitoring pay equity will help you implement your compensation strategy and address any issues before they become bigger problems.

Seven Questions to Ask for a Successful Compensation Strategy

Here are the things to think through when you are building a compensation strategy.

1. What Is Your Compensation Philosophy?

Start with your compensation philosophy.[2] Identify the principles and practices your organization uses to make compensation decisions:

- Do you generally make offers at the midpoint of the market rate for that role, or is it usually higher or lower? Why?

- What are the important considerations for how you determine incentive pay, and how do you allocate incentive and base pay?
- What consideration do you give benefits, leave, bonuses, and perks when you make decisions on wages?

The focus should be on why you pay people what you pay and what factors are important in how your total compensation is structured.[3]

2. Is Your Compensation Philosophy Working?

You can always do more of what you've been doing. But before you make that the default, it's worth understanding whether it's working. Before you start making compensation decisions, it's good to get a clearer picture of some key indicators:

- Track your turnover by role. Are you seeing higher than normal attrition?

- Look at average tenure by role. Is it trending longer or shorter? Do you know why?

- Are there gender pay gaps or other pay equity issues? When was your last pay equity audit?

- What's happening with employee engagement? Look deeper than the overall scores. Engagement data by department or demographic can reveal insights on where there are issues.

If you find potential issues, evaluate what role, if any, compensation is playing in employee satisfaction and turnover.

3. Are You Monitoring Compliance?

There are some aspects of compensation that are required by law and not optional. Understanding and monitoring compliance with compensation laws should be an essential part of any compensation strategy:

- Have you met minimum wage, overtime, and payment require-ments under local, state, and federal law for every location you have employees?
- Have you assessed pay equity and established a process to analyze and address any pay gaps?
- Are you up to date on new laws and changes regarding sick leave, parental leave, and other paid leave; pay transparency requirements; and other laws affecting compensation and payroll including laws on privacy and the transfer of data about employees?

4. Does Your Compensation Align with Business Strategy?

This is where you look at where the organization wants to go and what resources are allocated to getting there:

- What are the measurable goals for the company?
- Do you have the people you need to get the work done?
- Is there budget available to make sure you can hire and retain the people you need for the work? If not, identify gaps and what it takes to close them.

If there is a significant mismatch between goals and compensation budget, then you need to adjust one or the other or both.

5. Does Your Compensation Align with the Market?

Assessing how your pay compares with similar organizations will tell you if your compensation budget is realistic and competitive:

- Are your current salary ranges competitive for your location and industry?
- In a rapidly shifting environment, are you prepared to make adjustments?
- How do proposed changes affect pay equity?

If your compensation is not competitive, you will need to figure out how to adjust budget or headcount and get creative with benefits and other aspects of total compensation.

6. How Does Employee Performance Fit into Your Compensation Strategy?

There is a bit of a myth that if employees meet goals and perform at or above expectations, they should get a raise each year. That's not always possible and often not how it works. There are many types of incentive pay designed to encourage certain performance besides annual raises or cost-of-living adjustments:

- Can you create bonuses tied to performance or meeting specific goals?
- Is your sales commission program effective?
- Do you have the right mix of base pay and incentive pay?
- Do you use vesting of stock options or other benefits to encourage retention?

7. How Does Total Compensation Fit into Your Strategy?

Money is not always the most important thing to people. Scheduling, the ability to work remotely, paid time off, signing bonuses, and help with retirement savings or student loan payments can all change the equation for potential and existing employees:

- Do you know what matters most to your employees?
- What benefits are used the most?
- What else could you offer that might make a difference to people you want to recruit or retain?

While money is always an important factor, there are many other aspects of total compensation that can make your organization stand out against the competition. Know what they are and regularly reevaluate what's possible.

Building a successful compensation strategy is about having the right information on your organization, the market, and the organization's goals, then determining what's working, determining what isn't, and exploring options.

Twenty Building Blocks of a Great Compensation Strategy

1. **Competitive Pay Structure**: This ensures that employee salaries are at or above market value, which helps attract and retain top talent.
2. **Variable Pay**: These are performance-related incentives that encourage and reward top performers, such as bonuses or stock options.
3. **Equal Pay**: Ensure pay equity across genders, races, and other demographic groups to maintain fairness and compliance with legislation.
4. **Benefits Package**: This encompasses noncash compensation such as health insurance, retirement contributions, and paid time off, which can be major factors in attracting and retaining employees.
5. **Career Development Opportunities**: These can include training, education, and promotion opportunities, which can both improve employee skill sets and increase job satisfaction.
6. **Clear Communication**: Transparently communicating about compensation plans helps employees understand how their pay is determined and what they can do to increase it.
7. **Pay for Performance**: Linking pay increases directly to performance evaluations can incentivize employees to strive for excellence in their work.
8. **Legal Compliance**: Ensure that all aspects of the compensation strategy comply with local, state, and federal laws to avoid potential litigation and penalties.

9. **Regular Market Evaluation**: Continual benchmarking of your compensation strategy against market standards helps ensure that your pay remains competitive.

10. **Flexibility**: A great compensation strategy should be flexible enough to adapt to changes in business needs, market conditions, and individual employee situations.

11. **Geographic Differential**: Consider the cost of living and market rates in different locations where employees are based.

12. **Recognition Programs**: Implementing programs that recognize and reward employees for their contributions beyond what's expected, like employee of the month awards, can boost morale.

13. **Profit Sharing Plans**: These can provide employees with a share of the company's profits, creating a sense of ownership and aligning their interests with those of the company.

14. **Work–Life Balance**: Incorporating flexibility around work hours or providing remote work options can improve employee satisfaction and productivity.

15. **Job Evaluation**: This is a systematic way of determining the value or worth of a job in relation to other jobs in the organization, which helps establish a fair compensation system.

16. **Relocation Assistance**: If employees are expected to move for their job, offering relocation assistance can be an important part of the compensation strategy.

17. **Severance Pay**: Clear policies around severance pay can make transitions easier when layoffs or terminations are necessary.

18. **Retirement Plans**: Offering strong retirement or pension plans can attract mature professionals and encourage long-term commitment.

19. **Compensation Transparency**: This involves not just communication but also openness about how compensation is decided at every level, which can foster trust.

20. **Total Rewards Statement**: This communication tool provides employees with complete visibility of their compensation including salary, benefits, perks, and nonmonetary rewards.

How Compensation Policies Promote Pay Equity

by Sarah Morgan

Once the organization has established a compensation strategy, a compensation policy is the ideal way for the organization to ensure that pay equity practices are defined and infused in the organization. The compensation policy should be written and shared freely with employees and those seeking employment with the organization. The organization should not restrict access to the compensation policy such that employees are not clear on its existence or how it is applied. The organization should not weaponize the compensation policy against employees by only allowing limited access to it during complaint investigation or other contentious moments.

A compensation policy describes the details of how compensation is handled within an organization. It should include an overview of the organization's philosophy and strategy surrounding pay. This allows the organization to clearly express its commitment to compliance with all laws and guidelines relating to pay as well as its commitment to equal pay and to pay equity. It also allows the organization to share insight into how initial pay determinations are made for new hires, to describe how pay increases are determined relating to performance and promotion, and to advise existing employees on how to make inquiries about pay-related concerns. Most importantly, the compensation policy should provide the pay ranges for all positions in the company with indicators on how education, prior related work experience, and tenure will be weighted and factored into decisions related to pay.

Most organizations fail to create a written compensation policy. Instead, they use informal pay practices and rely on general pay decision precedent to guide decisions about compensation. This approach creates an opportunity for pay inequity and other unfair pay practices to become rampant in the organization. It also leaves the organization more open to liability and litigation. Therefore, this approach alone is not a recommended best practice.

When an organization does create a written policy, that policy is often held under the strictest confidence such that most employees in the organization never see it or may not even believe it exists. Worse, the organization may only share the policy in quoted snippets to defend and justify pay-related decisions arising from an employee question about or challenge to the pay practice. This kind of defensiveness and weaponizing of policy against employees is not aligned with a commitment to DEI in the workplace. It is not aligned with a commitment to compensation transparency or pay equity. This approach is also not a recommended best practice.

Compensation transparency requires willing and open sharing of the organization's philosophy, strategy, and policy with those currently or previously employed by the organization as well as those considering employment with the organization. It also includes a willingness to share with other third parties and potentially the public, if necessary, to demonstrate, defend, and/or maintain the integrity of the commitment to transparency and equity.

If an organization has not yet established a written compensation philosophy, strategy, and policy, it can still communicate transparently about how it handles compensation. While having a written, published policy is ideal and a best practice, it is also important to remember that DEI strategy is not an all-or-nothing game. It is not a game at all. It is a commitment to continuous improvement in the core areas arising from the intersection of the work and life of the people in the organization.

Here a few examples of ways that organizations can communicate transparently about compensation until it establishes a full, comprehensive written compensation policy:

- **Job postings**. Include pay amounts in both internal and external job postings. People deserve to know what a job is likely to pay them before choosing to apply or interview. This allows the individual to self-select out of opportunities that are unlikely to meet their personal financial needs. It also allows potential candidates and current employees to see that the organization is not afraid of sharing general information about compensation. It also gives employees who are considering applying for an internal lateral or upward position the ability to see paths for growth within the organization.

- **Why You Pay This Amount**. Explain how the salary amount was determined during the job offer process and/or in the offer letter. Adding a paragraph or table to explain in more specific detail how the salary amount being offered was determined goes a very long way in showing that the organization is committed to being open, transparent, and accountable for their pay choices and decisions. This explanation should include an overview of how much of the salary is the base pay for the position, how much is consideration for prior experience and/or education, how much is consideration for the market or geographic area, and so on. This information can be provided either as amounts or as percentages of the total salary.

- **Explain Total Compensation**. Provide compensation statements that include a breakdown of how the employee's current salary was determined and a listing of the compensation of others in related departments or positions. Compensation statements are a standard report in many HR and payroll systems. These statements typically include the salary the employee receives and the taxes remitted connected to the employee as well as company expenses relating to health benefits, retirement, and other perks. Less frequently, these statements include similar information about others in the same department or comparable positions. This allows employees to see not only the financial commitment the organization has given to them but what it has given to others and how employees fit into the bigger picture. Since health benefits, retirement matching, and employee perk contributions are typically flat amounts or percentages that are the same for each employee, the organization is easily able to demonstrate fairness and equity in sharing this information.

- **How to Get to the Next Level**. Explain how pay changes are determined when pay increases are given and share a listing of the compensation of others in related departments or positions. Sometimes pay changes are connected to a very specific event like a milestone of time with the organization or a promotion to a new position with greater responsibilities. Sometimes pay changes are awarded based on more seemingly arbitrary reasons related to performance or other outside accomplishment. Regardless of the reason, when a pay change is made, the individual impacted by the change should be notified why the change is happening, what the amount represents, and how the change impacts the earnings parity of the individual with others in the same department and comparable positions.

- **Be Transparent**. Allow employees the opportunity to make appointments to review the compensation information for themselves and those in comparable positions where they can ask clarifying questions. At some point during their employment with the organization, most employees are going to have questions or concerns about how they are being compensated in comparison to others in their department and comparable positions. Organizations committed to pay transparency and equity welcome the opportunity to discuss and explain this to their employees. These organizations normalize conversations around pay as being customary and typical in the employer–employee relationship. Therefore, these organizations create time and space to have open dialogue about pay-related decisions.

- **Show Your Pay Is Competitive**. Share periodic updates about wages for similar jobs and industries in the area. Organizations will either lead, loom, or lag the market in compensation. Leading the market means paying more than the average salary for a similar position, either slightly or significantly. Looming the market means paying exactly the average salary for a similar position. Lagging the market means paying less than the average salary for a similar position, either slightly or significantly. The decision of organizations to lead, loom, or lag is generally based on the revenue and expenses—or what the organization can afford—and the importance and/or likelihood of the position helping the organization achieve more revenue. In this way, the organization places a greater value on some positions over others. This is often an uncomfortable admission for an organization to make, and its decision to limit the sharing of pay information is, in part, its attempt to control the message surrounding this issue. Embracing pay equity and transparency requires organizations to lean into this discomfort in being more open about this fact. Alongside leaning into this discomfort, organizations can also share with their employees and those seeking employment within their organization how the pay for its positions compares to that of its competitors in the market. This kind of analysis also helps the organization make sure it maintains wages that are appropriate for the duties of the role, for the organization's industry, and for the area where its employees work and live.

It is important to note that, even if the organization does not choose to share this information with its employees, organizations should complete a salary benchmarking study or review. This is the process of matching internal jobs with salary survey results for the same or similar jobs within the organization's geographic area and national industry to learn how the salaries the organization is paying measure in comparison. A salary benchmarking study is how organizations determine if its awarded compensations are leading, looming, or lagging the market.

In furthering a commitment to DEI, closing the wage gap, and achieving equity, organizations should also study the cost of living in the geographic areas where the organization operates and where the employees live. It is not uncommon for an organization to pay wages that are competitive within the market and industry but still leave its employees unable to support themselves reasonably and fully. We will explore later in this chapter the impact of this on employees in more detail. However, it is important to note here that paying wages that leave employees unable to live a full, healthy lifestyle is contrary to the principles of DEI. Without these kinds of studies, the organization cannot be sure its wages are appropriate, and its commitment to pay equity and DEI becomes insincere and incomplete.

How Pay Equity Gets Out of Balance

by Sarah Morgan

Once an organization's compensation strategy and policies are in place, the work is not done. Change is a constant in organizations, and each new hire or person leaving can shift the balance.

Pay equity is most likely to fall out of balance when there are:

- **Many New Hires and Promotions**. When an organization is quickly bringing people onboard or promoting/moving them to new positions, it is easy to lose sight of appropriate and fairness with pay. This is particularly true when the organization is being negatively impacted by not having people employed and actively working in those roles. We have seen this in real time during the COVID-19 pandemic and what has been deemed "the Great Resignation." Staffing shortages have crippled many businesses such that they are willing to pay extraordinary amounts to fill their open positions. Over time, this approach will have a negative effect on the organization's ability to maintain pay equity.

- **Acquisitions and Mergers**. When two organizations come together to become one, the resulting organization will likely have employees holding similar job titles and roles with very different pay rates. The organization will have to decide how and when to address this to maintain fairness and equity in its pay practices.

- **Layoffs**. When an organization has to reduce its staff size, it will likely assign additional work to the employees who remain. If the organization is having a financial hardship, the employees may accept the additional work without expecting or demanding additional compensation at first. However, this will not last forever. As the organization recovers, those employees will be looking for additional compensation for the additional work that they are now responsible for. Organizations committed to pay equity and DEI will award the additional compensation as soon as financially possible. Failing to do this is likely to result in turnover or slowed production from employees negatively impacted by the decision. It is also likely to cause the organization to lag the market in compensation and have difficulty hiring new talent when needed.

- **Catastrophic Events**. Whether it is a global pandemic or a natural disaster like a hurricane, earthquake, or wildfire, a catastrophic event causes disruptions to the workplace that impact compensation in both the short and long term. Organizations must be prepared to address this with mercy and fairness. Organizations also have to recognize that how they address these issues is likely to disrupt pay equity if not monitored.

There are several ways pay gaps can be revealed outside of a traditional audit:

- **Third–Party Inquiry**. This kind of inquiry would come from a government agency or from an attorney representing an employee or group of employees. Organizations typically have little option but to respond fully and formally to a request from such a third party about its pay practices.
- **Employee Complaint**. This kind of inquiry would come from a current employee or employees of the organization. Typically, the employee will contact their supervisor or HR department stating they have learned another individual in the same or similar position as theirs is being paid more, and the individual wants to know if this is true and, if true, why this is the case. Many organizations choose not to respond to this kind of inquiry because it is not appropriate and possibly unlawful to discuss an employee's compensation with their coworker. Organizations continue to discourage employees from discussing compensation with each other for this reason, even though this kind of discouragement is unlawful.

    When this kind of inquiry is brought to the organization's attention, it should investigate and respond. This is how best to demonstrate commitment to pay equity and compensation transparency. The organization does not have to disclose the specifics of another employee's earnings to give a response. As mentioned previously in this section, it can provide a breakdown of how the employee's current salary was determined and a listing of the compensation of others in related departments or positions.

- **Workplace Rumors**. Despite how uncomfortable this makes the organization and no matter how often the organization discourages participation in such discussions, employees are going to talk about and compare their compensation. This is their right under the law in most places around the world, both professionally and personally. In participating in this kind of chatter, it is not uncommon for rumors about pay disparity to get back to members of management or HR. If this occurs, the organization can choose to respond. This response can include contacting some or all of the employees reportedly involved in the disruption to ask them to share their concerns so the organization can address those concerns. Another option would be to provide a listing of the compensation of those in the departments, locations, and the like involved in the meeting to all the employees in those areas. A final option would be to share the listing across the organization.

Pay equity should be part of compensation strategy and policies because it is far easier to plan for, budget, and maintain equitable pay than make up for pay gaps at the last minute.

Elements of a Great Compensation Plan

As you think about developing a compensation plan, here are the elements to consider. If you need help, call in a knowledgeable compensation consultant to help you develop a plan that works within your organizational structure and budget and helps you achieve your goals.

- **Competitive Salary Structure**. A competitive salary structure is one that is in line with industry standards and is attractive enough to retain top talent. A great compensation plan should include a salary structure that is competitive and fair.
- **Bonus Structure That Rewards Performance**. A bonus structure that rewards performance can be a great way to motivate employees and encourage them to work harder. A great compensation plan should include a bonus structure that is tied to performance and is fair.
- **Long-Term Incentive Plan That Gives Employees a Stake in the Company's Future**. A long-term incentive plan can help you retain employees over time by giving them a stake in the company's future. A great compensation plan should include a long-term incentive plan that is tied to the company's success.
- **Professional Development Opportunities**. Professional development opportunities can help you ensure that your employees are growing and developing their skills over time. A great compensation plan should include professional development opportunities that are tailored to each employee's needs.
- **Long-Term Benefits**. Long-term benefits are also important because they help you retain employees over time. A great compensation plan should include long-term benefits such as retirement plans, health insurance, and more.
- **Flexible Work Schedules and Vacations**. Work schedule and vacations are important because they help you ensure that your employees have a good work-life balance. A great compensation plan should include work schedules and vacation policies that are flexible and accommodating.
- **Health Insurance**. Health insurance is important because it helps you ensure that your employees have access to quality healthcare.

A great compensation plan should include health insurance policies that are comprehensive and affordable.

- **Miscellaneous Benefits**. Miscellaneous benefits can include things like tuition reimbursement, employee discounts, and more. A great compensation plan should include miscellaneous benefits that are tailored to each employee's needs.
- **Retirement Plan**. Finally, a retirement plan is important because it helps you ensure that your employees are prepared for retirement. A great compensation plan should include retirement plans that are comprehensive and affordable.

What separates a great compensation plan from an average one is how well it meets the needs of both the employer and the employee. An average compensation plan may be adequate, but it won't necessarily attract or retain top talent. A great compensation plan will be tailored to the needs of both parties and will be designed to help the company succeed over the long term.

CHAPTER 5

How to Audit Pay Equity

by Kent Plunkett

Assessing and improving pay equity has become easier as tech companies have developed tools to help organizations understand pay practices both internally and in the market. It's now possible to assess pay equity in your organization, identify potential issues, and have the information you need to address any gaps. With that in mind, we define pay equity as follows:

> *Equal pay for comparable work that is internally equitable, externally competitive, and transparently communicated.*

This holistic view of pay equity shifts compensation analysis from pure market pricing to a broader equity approach that is sustainable, fair, and designed for business success.

The Plunkett Pay Equity Framework has six steps to guide you from organizational commitment to pay equity all the way to a pay equity practice that will keep you compliant, competitive, and fair.

Step 1: Secure a Leadership Mandate

The first step is to secure a leadership mandate. This requires more than a nod or an approval. It's a commitment to an equitable pay philosophy. Your pay philosophy should do the following:

- State that pay equity is mandated by both your leadership team and board of directors.
- Communicate that your leadership team is working continuously to ensure a balance between external competitiveness and internal equity.
- Outline your organization's commitment to transparent communication.

You also need the right resources, which include people and budget. Most leaders want to understand what you want to do and why, how it will benefit the organization, how much time it will take, and what it costs. Familiarize yourself with the process and information in this book and talk to a compensation consultant and/or your pay equity solution provider so you are prepared to answer all these questions.

You may want to start with a pay equity audit by a compensation expert to set the baseline and identify potential gaps. That way, you can demonstrate the need for ongoing analysis and monitoring as a compliance issue as well as a fairness and competitiveness issue.

Because pay equity is based on comparing people's compensation and work, it can change every time an employee is hired or leaves. You need someone to continually monitor pay equity. This is often done with attorneys who can advise the organization on risks and strategy while protecting the confidentiality of the process. None of this can happen without senior leadership's understanding and commitment to a fair and competitive compensation philosophy and the resources to create and maintain equitable pay practices.

Step 2: Group Comparable Jobs

Doing a pay equity analysis is not just about equal pay; it's also about equal work. Since no two jobs are exactly alike, no jobs are ever equal in practice. So we break each role down into component parts or attributes, then we compare those factors to see where things are alike and different. The idea is to end up with groups of similar roles that have similar skills, effort, responsibility, and working conditions.

Be Careful How You Compare

If we wanted to compare desserts, we could look at calories; weight; volume; and the breakdown of fat, carbs, and protein. But none of that really matters when you are choosing between apple pie and chocolate chip cookies. You already know what you're going to choose because of your experience tasting them and your preferences about pie, apples, cookies, and chocolate.

This is why it's essential to keep the problem you're trying to solve in front of you while you select the attributes to compare. It's tempting to choose attributes you can measure easily or use some data that you already have. It's harder to make sure that what you are comparing will give you useful information for what you want to know or do.

The temptation here is to start with jobs in similar pay ranges since they should theoretically reflect the value of different jobs to the organization. The problem is that this approach skips analyzing the work itself. You don't want to assume that jobs are similar based on their pay; they need to be comparable based on the work.

That said, most organizations have hierarchies based loosely on skills, effort, and especially responsibility, and pay generally correlates with the hierarchy. So, as you go through the process of grouping comparable jobs, you may see them cluster by pay range. If so, it's a sign your compensation structure has a good foundation for pay equity. But it does not mean you can skip comparing the actual work; the people doing that work; and whether there are pay gaps connected to gender, race, or other factors that could reveal bias.

How to Compare Jobs for Pay Equity

Pay equity laws require us to compare jobs by comparing level of skills, effort, responsibility, and working conditions. You are determining "comparable work" or "substantially similar work"; they mean the same thing.

Skills refer to the ability to do a specific task; the ability to use certain tools or software effectively; or broader abilities like creativity, writing, analysis, or even understanding of quantum physics. The key to comparing skills is being able to effectively describe the actual work that people do in the job and the abilities needed to do it.

Effort is how hard the work is. Effort includes the physical, mental, and emotional capacities needed for the job. While being a therapist does not require physical effort, the mental and emotional energy required to do the work is significant. Being a teacher, a doctor, or a firefighter involves all three. When comparing effort, it's important to consider the emotional work and the cumulative effect of work that requires more than one form of effort.

Responsibility is often expressed as how many people have either solid or dotted lines to you as their leader in the organization chart. But having people report to you is just part of assessing responsibility. It also involves understanding the role's value and importance to the organization. This can be hard to both quantify and describe. The truth is that it takes many talented people to support leaders and get the work done. We've all had experiences where it didn't matter that much when the boss was gone, but when her assistant was out, everything started to fall apart. But the analysis of responsibility is about who is, well, responsible. To determine responsibility, look at who has the ultimate accountability for the work rather than who actually makes it happen.

Working conditions include the environmental, practical, or other physical conditions that make the work more challenging or difficult. A marine scientist in the Arctic works in dramatically different conditions from one in the Caribbean. Schedules such as night shifts or exposure to constant noise, heat, cold, or hazardous conditions all make a difference in the actual work and usually the pay associated with that work.

In looking at pay equity, we first compare jobs so we can later compare pay for those jobs. When there are disparities in pay between similar jobs (and there usually are), we compare the people doing those jobs to understand their differences. If one person is making more because they have more experience, special training, or other factors, then the pay difference may be justified.

Collect the Right Data

To do a pay equity analysis, you will need job data, pay data, and people data.

Job data. Useful data about your organization's jobs requires more than simply matching job titles or making assumptions about skills and effort based on where the role fits in the organization chart. Start with job descriptions that have information on

- Skills needed to perform the work,
- Duties,
- Training and certifications,
- Education requirements,
- Experience required for the work,
- Technical proficiency,
- Physical requirements,
- Mental and emotional requirements,
- Management competencies, and
- General working conditions.

If your job descriptions need work, you are not alone. It's common for organizations to look at their job descriptions and realize they were created for recruiting or workers' compensation. Often this is the biggest lift in preparing for a pay equity analysis—describing the work in the needed categories in words that are consistent in meaning so that comparison is possible.

There are tools that can help you create and maintain job descriptions that you can use for pay equity and everything else.

It is worth the time and effort to update your job descriptions and have consistent language to describe the work. It not only makes pay equity analysis easy but also provides valuable and useful information for recruiting, career development, and workforce planning.

Compensation data. Compensation data should include

- Salary/pay rate,
- Bonuses,
- Commissions,
- Other forms of incentive pay, and
- Any other pay additions.

If most people have the same benefits, then you can ignore the value of benefits. But if benefits are significantly different in different areas of the organization, it is good to have these data available as well because it may affect the comparison of pay and can be useful to assess pay differences after the pay equity audit.

People data. The pay equity audit process first compares the work and pay for that work. Then it looks at whether there are aspects of the people in those roles that affect pay. You need data that can help determine if there are pay gaps related to a protected class. You also want to understand differences in pay between people doing similar jobs but making different compensation to see if it makes sense based on your compensation strategy. People data should include

- Demographic data on
  - Gender,
  - Race,
  - Age,
  - Ethnicity,

- o Disability, and
- o Other protected factors such as veteran status; and
- Employee data that includes
  - o Tenure at organization,
  - o Time in position,
  - o Performance ratings,
  - o Relevant job experience,
  - o Relevant education or training, and
  - o Specific job qualifications such as licenses or certifications.

Evaluate Jobs and Create Job Structure

Once you have the data you need, you can start the job evaluation process to determine the relative worth of the jobs and create an internally aligned job structure. Compare jobs according to their relative skill, effort, and responsibilities and group the ones that are similar. Then look at how the work adds value and helps the organization achieve its goals.

This process should result in a job-worth hierarchy that ranks jobs based on skills, duties, responsibilities, and value to the organization. When deciding on how many levels to define, make sure you don't get so specific that multiple levels end up with only one or two jobs. You also don't want to be so general that, when you look at pay ranges for the group, the range is so wide it's almost meaningless.

What you want is a structure that has clear criteria and enough detail to make meaningful decisions about compensation for your organization. It's common to find roles that don't quite fit into any group and to decide to group jobs that seem pretty different in practice. Don't get too hung up on specific details of the work. It's okay to group dissimilar jobs together if they require comparable levels of responsibility, effort, and abilities. You really are comparing apples and oranges, but it's okay to call them all fruit.

While grouping comparable jobs involves the most work, it's also the foundation for everything that follows. It's worth taking the time, validating the data, and making thoughtful and informed decisions on what makes jobs the same or different.

Create Your Job Descriptions

Here are some places to start with your job descriptions.

Job families and pay bands. Start with job families and pay bands. A job family is a group of jobs that involve similar work and require similar training, skills, knowledge, and expertise. Job families help organizations compare and organize related jobs across different departments or divisions. They can also aid in determining the primary job duties and career progression opportunities within an organization.

Pay bands, also known as salary ranges, are scopes that illustrate the ideal salaries employers can pay employees for their positions. Pay bands include the minimum and maximum amount of money a company can afford to dedicate to compensation. They are based on factors like location, experience, or seniority and help promote pay equity, transparency, and clear salary outlines for new candidates.

Ten Steps to Find and Eliminate Bias in Job Descriptions

Creating bias-free job descriptions is an important part of promoting diversity, equity, and inclusion in the workplace. Here are ten steps you can follow to create bias-free job descriptions:

1. **Review the Job Requirements**: Start by reviewing the actual job requirements and qualifications needed for the role. Ensure that these requirements are truly necessary for success in the position and remove any unnecessary or biased criteria.
2. **Use Gender-Neutral Language**: Avoid gendered pronouns and terms in the job description. Instead of using "he" or "she," use gender-neutral pronouns like "they" or rephrase the sentences to avoid pronouns altogether.
3. **Focus on Essential Functions**: Clearly outline the essential functions and responsibilities of the job. Ensure that these functions are based on objective criteria and are necessary for success in the role.

4. **Avoid Overly Specific Language**: Use language that is inclusive and avoids unnecessary specificity. Instead of using terms like "rockstar" or "ninja," which can be gendered or culturally biased, focus on describing the skills and abilities required.

5. **Eliminate Discriminatory Language**: Avoid any language that may discriminate against or discourage certain groups of people. For example, avoid using words that may imply age, race, religion, or disability bias.

6. **Highlight Diversity and Inclusion**: Explicitly state your commitment to diversity and inclusion in the job description. Emphasize that the company values and welcomes candidates from diverse backgrounds.

7. **Use Inclusive Terminology**: Instead of using terms that may be biased or exclusionary, opt for inclusive language. For example, use terms like "strong collaborator" instead of "team player" to avoid gender stereotypes.

8. **Focus on Transferable Skills**: Instead of placing undue emphasis on specific job titles or industry experience, focus on transferable skills and abilities that can be applied to the role. This opens up opportunities for candidates from diverse backgrounds.

9. **Provide Flexibility**: Consider offering flexible work arrangements or alternative qualifications that would allow a wider range of candidates to apply. This can help attract candidates who may have different life circumstances or nontraditional career paths.

10. **Seek Diverse Perspectives**: Involve a diverse group of employees or stakeholders in the review process to ensure that the job description is unbiased. They can provide valuable input and help identify any potential biases that may have been overlooked.

Step 3: Model Internal Equity

The next step is to see where there may be pay gaps by running a multivariate regression analysis of your pay data based on different demographic factors. A multivariate regression is not what happens when everyone comes home for the holidays. It's a statistical analysis that compares things to see whether and how they are related. For pay equity, the multivariate regression compares pay and work with demographic data such as gender, race, age, tenure, or any other variable you want to explore. This is the kind of work computers are really good at doing. What you get is a chart or model that shows where pay gaps exist and whether they are correlated to any of the demographic factors such as race, age, and gender.

If you see potential pay equity issues, you then do a deeper review, or a cohort analysis, in those areas to see whether the pay gaps can be justified by legitimate business reasons or whether they reveal bias. This is also the place to test potential issues with your data. For example, if the factors you analyzed don't explain the pay differences, you may want to assess whether you are using the right job groups. Any time the results are strange or surprising, check your data first.

The cohort analysis is also where you evaluate factors that are permissible reasons for paying people differently such as tenure, experience, and qualifications. You are trying to figure out a statistical connection between reasons that could explain the pay differences you uncover.

If you identify pay gaps that may need adjusting, you can also use multivariate regression analysis to model what would happen if you increased pay in the areas where there appear to be gaps. Sometimes, this will cause issues in other groups. To determine how your proposed pay increases affect pay equity overall, run the regression analysis again for the entire organization and see what happens.

At this point, it's also good to get your employment attorneys involved to help you understand where there are potential pay equity issues and get their help and advice. It can also protect your discussions of any problems and strategies for remediation under the attorney-client and/or work product privileges. Your multivariate regression results can give you a good picture of potential pay gaps and what factors they are statistically connected to. By looking deeper, you can see where you may have problems and test possible solutions.

Step 4: Benchmark External Competitiveness

After you complete your internal pay equity analysis in Step 3, then it's time to look to see how your organization's compensation compares to compensation in the market for specific jobs. This is also called benchmarking. It's a funny term that has nothing to do with a long seat. It's an old surveying term for the mark made on a stone to show where to install the bracket, or bench, to hold measuring equipment.

It's important to go through the benchmarking process before you make any decisions on compensation because you may find additional areas to adjust. And any adjustments can affect pay equity in other places.

Benchmarking accuracy depends on the work you have done in describing your organization's jobs and the quality and availability of outside data on similar jobs. If you do it right, you will get an accurate assessment of how your organization's pay compares to your competitors.

If everyone works remotely, benchmark based on your industry, size of organization, and roles. If employees generally work on site or are hybrid, you will also want to look at compensation in your geographic location(s). In both cases, you want specific job information so you can make the most accurate comparisons instead of guessing whether the market jobs are comparable. Some market pricing best practices include the following:

- Choose the compensation survey data relevant to your jobs. WorldatWork recommends that 50 percent of your company jobs should be market priced.
- Compare the minimum requirements of the job itself rather than the qualifications of a particular employee.
- A good "match" is when at least 80 percent of the duties are similar.
- For jobs that don't have enough information to compare, look at similar levels of skill, knowledge, effort, and responsibility. Or you can "slot" the job between two survey jobs that the role might fall between.

You Probably Have Issues, but They May Not Be the Ones You Expect

In dealing with pay equity analytics, cohort construction is vital. Determining which similarly situated roles belong in a grouping includes reviewing role responsibilities, organizational control, and competency applications. It's not for the faint of heart!

In working with an enterprise organization with almost 25,000 employees, my team was tasked with such an analysis for cohorts. One of the primary reasons for the pay equity analysis was to affirm their values-based approach to talent. There was a certain way the organization worked, and they espoused these value-laden approaches often. They had a mild concern that perhaps there was compensation disbursement misalignment at a mid-tier career level or two.

When we confirmed cohorts and began our regression-based analysis, we found very few reasons to be concerned at that mid-tier level. Despite the inconsistent manner for raises and promotion, which did need to be addressed, they fell into accidental affirmation in their standard deviation about 92 percent of the time. Not bad!

Where I knocked them off of their chairs, however, was upon review of the executive-level cohort. Despite being wonderfully inclusive of gender at that level, those who identified as female where trending far below their male counterparts in the regression models. The ultimate truth exposed during the analysis was that the longer females stayed with the organization, the more inequitable their pay became. "Punished for loyalty" was not a value that the organization had nor was it one that they wanted to be identified by talent within the company. Truth be told, the board of the organization was a bit heartsick at what the math showed.

The next bitter bill to swallow, however, was the approach and timeline to course correction. It was likely at 12–16-month process of equitable alignment with a spend of just over a million dollars. The tension in those meetings was real as leadership was faced with a look in the mirror—are we who we say we are and are we willing to pay to affirm who we say we are. Definitely a rubber meeting the road time for that leadership, but in the end, they developed a plan and budgeting to address the inequity.

Values will cost you something or they are likely not values. Pay equity analytics will help to reveal those real values. Math does not lie.

—John Baldino, MSHRD SPHR SHRM-SCP
President, Humareso

As you can imagine, it's unusual to exactly match jobs at your organization with jobs at other organizations. So there is an art to benchmarking external competitiveness. Familiarity with the work, roles, and industry helps. It's also important to know and understand your organization's compensation philosophy and strategy so that, when you get the benchmarking data, you are making compensation decisions that are consistent with the organization's overall goals and approach.

Step 5: Communicate Transparently

When an organization is transparent about pay, the positive impact on culture, employee engagement, productivity, and innovation can be profound. Communicate the outcome of your pay equity analysis and include resources for both managers and employees to understand what goes into compensation decisions. Your goal is to both educate and manage expectations. The most important part of communications about pay is not only to say that discussions about compensation are welcome but to mean it. This requires that managers understand the organization's compensation philosophy and have the information they need to discuss pay issues with their reports.

Components of a Communication Plan

As you develop your plan, think through whether people understand why they are paid what they are paid, think about what information they need, and offer guidance on how to have compensation conversations.

1. *Communicate Your Compensation Philosophy*
   Your compensation philosophy addresses what is rewarded and why. It provides guidance for compensation decisions so that they are made consistently using the same principles, instead of ad hoc as individuals are hired or promoted. A compensation philosophy is more than an EEO (equal opportunity employer) statement. Pay is a combination of individual qualifications and performance,

Talking About Pay Can Be Awkward

I had a *pay transparency* experience long before it was something to note and utilize as a good business practice.

In a past job, I was an HR department of one and part of the leadership team of a small entrepreneurial manufacturing company. We were loosely structured when it came to systems around people. This was true throughout the company. Compensation data and knowledge sat mostly with me in my role as HR Director. I'd share with the CEO and CFO but that was it.

During my time at the company, the CEO moved out of the day-to-day facets of the operation of the business to focus on new sales and business development. He named a new President who hadn't had much organizational exposure. He had been the head of engineering for decades, so this was a big shift for him personally and as a company.

(Remember we were an entrepreneurial group. We didn't have internal systems for development, promotions, role changes, etc. They just happened by decree.)

At a leadership gathering soon after the new President had taken the helm, he went off script from the meeting's agenda. I mean **WAY OFF SCRIPT!**

Out of nowhere, he paused the meeting and declared, "I'd like to bring something up. I don't know why Steve makes the salary he does."

He meant me. This wasn't one of those, "I have a friend, let's call him Steve," examples. He bowled right through the awkward pause and gasps from around the table. He kept on plowing, "I'd like an answer. I was reviewing salaries of all of the managers, and I thought his salary was out of line." (No context mind you.)

Again, no answers. No one knew what to say or how to broach the silence. He started to get visibly angry and red in the face. He then bellowed, "Someone answer me!"

The CEO calmly looked up and chimed in. "Larry, this may not be the place for this discussion. But, to make a point," he looked across the table at me, "Steve, answer him. How much do you make a year?"

My eyes bulged and I couldn't believe what I was being asked to share publicly. However, I trusted the CEO and knew he was going to use this as a learning experience for everyone in the room. I stammered and said, "Rich, I make $35,000/yr."

"Excellent," he replied. "Now, how much does Ron make?" Ron was the plant manager. I knew I had no choice but to respond. "Ron makes $60,000/yr." I stated a bit more confidently. You could sense how unbelievably uncomfortable this was for everyone. Rich didn't stop. He had me recite everyone's salary around the table one by one. This took about ten painstaking minutes until there were two people remaining.

I knew who the next request would be. "How much does Larry make as our new President?" I looked straight into Larry's eyes as I said, "Larry makes $150,000/ yr." Larry was about to explode seeing where this was going. "And me, Steve? How much do I make?" Rich asked. I hesitated. No one except me and the CFO knew Rich's salary. "Go ahead. It's safe," he assured me. "Um, you make $250,000/yr., Rich."

Rich then took control of the meeting. "From now on, I'm going to get the traditional leather letterman jackets and we'll publish everyone's salary on their sleeves. When they get a raise, we'll make sure to update them. How does that sound?"

No one responded. Larry was mortified. Rich did take this as a learning opportunity.

"Larry. Salaries are just numbers. You put value on them based on how you feel about each person. I'm sure that you're okay with every engineer's salary around the table because you work with them. You haven't worked directly with many of the non-engineering folks. However, you're judging them and what they make. That's not your role. That's one of the reasons I have Steve. We'll talk about this later to help give you context. Good?"

But it wasn't a request. It was a statement.

Pay transparency is a wonderful thing **IF** you keep in mind how emotional compensation is as a field, a topic, and as a system. Understand how to be transparent in your pay practices and data so that you are informing people. Also, make sure it serves as a measuring stick for your pay equity efforts. Those are healthy approaches. Don't use the Larry Method of pay as a weapon!

—Steve Browne, SHRM-SCP
Chief People Officer for LaRosa's, Inc.

the organization's overall performance, and market conditions. Explain how these factors go into compensation decisions and what the organization is doing to monitor and address pay equity.

2. *Explain How to Understand Job Descriptions and How Compensation Works*
Both employees and managers should be familiar with the pay ranges and compensation levels the organization uses. Job descriptions are an essential part of understanding how and why a job is at a certain level and range. This helps both managers and employees understand what skills the employee should be working on for promotion and to recognize opportunities for learning and growth. These discussions also help employees understand what compensation factors apply to everyone and what depends on the employee's performance.

3. *Train Managers on How to Communicate with Employees about Pay*
If you are just beginning to talk about compensation and pay equity, then start by training managers on the organization's pay philosophy, strategy, and practices. This will promote more consistent and equitable pay decisions and provide managers with the resources they need to have pay conversations with the people they supervise.

Managers need to understand how pay decisions get made and what matters in making those decisions. Each manager should be able to explain to employees why they are paid what they are paid, all of the factors that are considered in making compensation decisions, and what the employee can do to influence their pay. Managers also need to understand the organization's process for assessing and addressing pay equity, including how the organization monitors and evaluates pay equity. A pay equity analyst can support managers and others in the communication process with data and insights.

Training for managers should be ongoing so their ability to discuss pay with their employees becomes a core competency. In addition, when significant changes or transactions occur, such as a merger or acquisition, it's important to communicate the impact on your pay philosophy.

4. *Provide Resources for Employees to Understand Their Pay*
   Make understanding pay easy for employees. Provide an "Understanding Pay" resources section in your employee portal. This can include

   o Diagrams and information to understand their paycheck, benefits, and deductions;
   o A glossary of terms and definitions;
   o Questions to ask when choosing benefits;
   o What to consider in declaring dependents for taxes; and
   o Links to credible outside resources for additional research.

   Your "Understanding Pay" resource section can also include FAQs on the organization's pay philosophy and how those principles are put into practice. And be sure to list whom to contact in the organization for help.

   Then schedule regular check-ins between employees and managers to discuss pay and any questions the employee has. If you determine pay adjustments annually, be sure to schedule a check-in at least quarterly to help employees set realistic expectations and let them know what they can do to increase their pay in the short and longer terms.

   These issues can be complicated, especially if there is a major change on the horizon. Consider the messaging, timing, and how it will affect both employees and the organization. Internal communications often don't stay internal. It's important to make sure that what you are saying internally is consistent with what you want to say externally.

5. *Provide Total Compensation Statements*
   Total Compensation Statements explain an employee's pay and benefits and how their compensation compares to others in the organization. The statement should contain comprehensive information on all aspects of the employee's pay and benefits—from base pay and bonuses to medical insurance, 401(k), taxes, and any other benefits the employee receives. Total Compensation

Statements also include the pay range for the employee's role, their position-in-range (PIR), and the average PIR for other jobs at that grade. This information helps an employee understand how they fit into your internal structure, where they sit among their peers, and what opportunities exist for growth in the organization.

Total Compensation Statements should be part of every performance review and any discussion about pay adjustments. The statements should be updated and provided to employees at least quarterly. Some organizations incorporate them into the employee portal so employees can access them any time.

6. *Communicate the Organization's Performance on Pay Equity*

When you do a pay equity audit, announce that the company retained an outside expert to conduct an objective pay equity audit and certification. When the results are in and you have determined what the organization is going to do in response, communicate the plan, timelines, and who will be affected. Remind everyone that when a company makes pay equity adjustments, it can only give raises to address pay gaps and cannot lower anyone's pay.

If people have been discouraged from talking about pay in the past, assure employees that things are changing and the goal is to provide fair and equitable pay for all. This may result in requests for raises from people who would like more money but don't have the bigger picture on budget and what the organization is trying to achieve. If raises are not coming any time soon, let people know that. Otherwise, communications can backfire as the company makes a big announcement about pay equity while it appears to be doing nothing.

Pay transparency is an important part of building trust with employees and demonstrating the organization's commitment to advancement for all. Give people accurate information, set realistic expectations, and make sure your actions are consistent with your philosophy and communications.

7. *Measure Success*

How do you know if your pay equity efforts are working? Define what success looks like at the outset, determine your key performance metrics, and measure results regularly. Start by defining your goals. Are you addressing pay equity to simply reduce the likelihood of future litigation? Is your organization motivated by a desire to increase employee engagement and productivity? Create a strong employer brand that attracts and retains top talent? Positive financial outcomes? All of the above?

Next, define what a successful outcome looks like and identify the data you need to measure progress against your pay equity goals.

To find and keep the right people, measure the impact of pay on recruiting and retention to find and keep the right people.

- ○ Monitor voluntary turnover rates and conduct exit interviews to learn the extent to which pay was a deciding factor.
- ○ Measure win/loss rates and how often candidates decline job offers due to pay.

To monitor for signs of wage compression, define compensation targets across key foundational pay metrics and monitor closely. Wage compression happens when there is very little difference between employees' pay even when there should be based on their respective skills, knowledge, abilities, and experience. It usually happens when new hires are brought in at pay comparable to that of existing employees who have more experience.

To assess wage compression:

- ○ Evaluate market data to determine the *market rate* for your target employees and monitor your market-ratios to measure external equity and how competitive you are in recruiting talent.
- ○ Understanding salary *range placement* relative to the midpoint for each position will guide you as you set salaries for new hires or consider pay raises for existing employees.

o Also called the comparison ratio, the *compa-ratio* considers how much an employee is making and where their compensation falls compared to the midpoint of a salary range. Like range placement, the compa-ratio is a key metric in measuring pay equity.

o *Target percentile* is important when considering your organization's hiring needs. If your goal is to recruit top talent, then your target might be the 75th percentile of the pay range. Monitor your target percentiles and watch for signs of wage compression.

To understand employee engagement, monitor key performance indicators:

o Conduct polls or employee surveys to assess awareness and perceptions of your pay equity initiatives, attitudes, and engagement. The response rates can also tell you a lot. If no one is responding, there's something they don't want to say.

o Check Glassdoor ratings and comments.

o Look at whether voluntary turnover rates and absenteeism are going up.

o Measure productivity using work quality and quantity metrics such as revenue per employee and human capital return on investment.

o Consider quarterly polls for employees and key stakeholders to assess awareness and perceptions of your pay equity initiatives, attitudes, and engagement.

o Keep in mind that metrics help you gauge progress at a high level, but success is ultimately measured one employee at a time.

Step 6: Update Continuously

The thing about pay equity is that it is not something you can achieve, declare victory, and then comfortably rest on your great efforts and results. Pay equity is dynamic. The potential for pay gaps arises every time you hire someone, someone leaves, or there are changes to compensation like raises and bonuses.

This brings us to the final step of the Plunkett Pay Equity Framework, the one that never really ends: update your pay equity analysis throughout the year. It also means it's important to regularly review and update your job structures, job descriptions, and any other compensation data you use to determine hiring pay and raises or bonuses. The essence of Step 6 is lather, rinse, repeat.

If you are thinking this sounds like a lot of work, it all depends on your data and tools for reviewing and analyzing pay equity. It also depends on having a solid pay philosophy and strategy to lean on when your analysis shows that there are issues to look at further and address.

Using Pay Equity Software

by Steve Boese

Using programs designed to audit and monitor pay equity makes the entire process easier. The technical processes, the data to be included, and the cadence of internal progress reporting for the organization's pay equity program are subject to several factors.

First, the organization should evaluate the human capital management (HCM) reporting tools and capabilities they have. The expertise of internal staff who will be involved in the process and the ability of users to consume and interpret this information are also important. It could be that additional investments will be required in HCM reporting technology, additional training for staff and end users, or even budget to outsource or contract some or all the reporting tasks.

Next, the nature of the reporting, and the data to be included in reports, must be specified. As with other HR and employee reporting, the sensitivity of employee data and the security requirements around the data must be consistent with the organization's data privacy and security policies. Additionally, with compensation data, adequate measures must be taken to ensure that confidential employee information is not disclosed or can be determined in the pay equity reports and analyses.

Last, the cadence of pay equity reporting should be established and communicated throughout the organization. Whatever reporting schedule is developed, make sure it happens. This will instill accountability and create transparency, credibility, and trust in the overall pay equity program.

CHAPTER 6

After the Audit: How to Address Pay Equity

After completing a pay equity audit, most organizations find pay gaps and that they might have pay equity issues. Most organizations do, in fact, have pay equity problems. It's not your fault. It's what happens when many humans make lots of hiring decisions about other humans and jobs over time. And since pay equity changes every time pay decisions are made, there's no way to achieve perfection and keep it that way. Pay equity is not a solid state. What matters most is what you do next and how you handle it.

Attorneys Play an Important Role in Pay Equity

Any pay equity analysis involves judgment calls on how to group jobs and where people belong in pay ranges. When you find potential pay gaps, then you need to figure out whether those gaps are due to legitimate business reasons like one person having more experience or special training that justifies the pay difference. This also involves judgment calls.

Often there are potential pay equity issues with women and other marginalized groups making less for the same work. It isn't intentional, but it is real. You need someone who understands the issues and can help you make the judgment calls. You also need good advice from someone who can assess the legal and practical risks and guide you in determining what to do next. A good employment lawyer familiar with pay equity and discrimination law is a valuable partner in any pay equity analysis.

Maintain Confidentiality of the Audit Process and Results

When lawyers are involved in the process to give legal advice on how to compare comparable work and pay practices, understand and mitigate risk, and address any potential problems, the audit process is protected by the attorney-client and work product privileges. The underlying data about the work, pay, and people in the roles can still be discovered if there is litigation. But your analysis, thinking, exploration of options, and decision-making will be protected if there are pay equity claims that arise.

Bad Fixes Make Problems Worse

When addressing pay gaps, it's essential to understand how they affect everyone. If you give one person a raise to bring them into the pay range for the work, how does that affect other people at the low end of the same range? Do you end up with a situation where the new man is now making more than the women who have more experience? What if the new man is Hispanic and the women are Black, White, and both over 40? Does the pay make sense based on legitimate business reasons or does it appear that one group consistently makes more than others?

Even pay adjustments that seem equal can amplify bias. A 3 percent cost-of-living increase for everyone can effectively widen pay gaps. For example, a woman making $50,000 would receive a raise of $1,500. A man making $70,000 would get $2,100. Now, instead of a $20,000 pay difference, it's $20,600. And the difference widens over time whenever increases are based on a percentage of current salary.

Your employment attorney can help you walk through your pay practices and any proposed decisions and help you prevent making seemingly straightforward solutions into bigger problems.

Your Attorneys Are There to Help and Protect the Organization

Legal is known for saying no and worrying too much about scary things that may never happen. Attorneys are often perceived as an obstacle instead of a partner. Sometimes it's even true.

Why Confidentiality Matters

I was sitting in a room with my client's senior leadership to give them a status update on a discrimination issue I was advising them about. Of course, I can't tell you exactly what happened, or who was involved, but this is a fictional version that shows why talking to your friendly employment lawyer can be really important.

As we started to wrap up one of leaders said, "Hey, Kelly had her baby! She's planning to come back part-time for the first six months and we're not sure that's going to work. We don't have any other leaders who work part-time, and the bonus structure is based on both the performance of the company and full-time work by the leader. We were wondering if you've dealt with that before."

I asked some questions about the bonus structure and their concerns. It turned out that the bonus structure was easy to deal with. The real issue was the leaders' (mostly male) concerns about Kelly's commitment to the organization now that she had a baby.

The discussion continued as various leaders speculated about whether she would ever come back full-time and how many other kids she wanted. They were concerned about having her being involved in an upcoming, high profile event involving the department she led. "Who knows what might happen. We need to make sure there's consistency and the work gets done right." Then they began talking about Kelly's husband who was an executive in another company. One person wondered why Kelly would even come back to work at all since her husband made good money and she didn't really need to work.

These were well-meaning leaders who wanted to do the right thing for their organization. They had respect for Kelly and valued her as their colleague. They also had some outdated views of woman and work that they didn't even realize.

I asked whether the conversation would be the same if the employee had cancer or major surgery. Generally, the consensus is that they would not be discussing someone's desired number of children or how much money the employee's spouse makes.

We're human. We get things wrong. We can maintain outdated views on things until we have a chance to look at them in a different light. Having someone you trust in the room who is there to help you matters. The attorney-client privilege allows room to try out ideas, discuss pros and cons, and come up with strategies that are both legal and will work. But sometimes, it's messy getting there.

—Heather Bussing
California Employment Lawyer

But there are usually good reasons when attorneys are cautious. They are there to have your back, understand and address risk, and ensure compliance with laws you may not even know exist. Equally important is that preventing problems takes a lot less time and resources than dealing with them after it's too late.

Your legal team will try to understand what you want and need to do and help you navigate a path to accomplish your objectives. They are there to help you and the organization succeed at providing great products and services to your clients while helping create a great and fair place to work.

Are Your Pay Gaps Discrimination?

The results of a pay equity audit will identify statistical correlations between pay and members of a protected class. It tells you where women and people of color are paid less than others doing similar work. It does not tell you why. And correlation is not causation.[1]

To figure out whether the pay gaps are potential discrimination or can be justified based on legitimate business factors, you have to look at both the work and the individuals doing the work. Work is comparable for pay equity when it requires similar skills, effort, and responsibility and is done under similar working conditions. This is where you double check whether you grouped comparable jobs correctly. For example, if you are paying your office manager in Boston significantly more than the office manager in Omaha, it likely has to do with geographic location and cost of living, which are legitimate reasons for pay differences. And if you are paying your tech assistants differently, look at whether they are required to do calculus or make copies.

If the work is basically comparable (it won't ever be a perfect fit), next look at the people doing the work. See if the pay gap is related to specific skills, training, qualifications, certifications, or another factor that would justify paying one person more. This can include significant differences in experience or performance. It's a judgment call. But unless there is some factor that really stands out so that the reason for the pay gap is obvious, it's probably better to address the pay gap.

Closing the Pay Gap

When you close the pay gap, you eliminate the risk and don't have to spend any more time or stress trying to assess or justify the differences in things that are already hard to compare—like people and their work.

If you are using software that helps assess pay equity, it will probably give you the amounts it will take to close the pay gaps you find. It's a good idea to see the costs involved before you spend too much time and money trying to justify the gaps. It may be cheaper to simply close the gaps if the work and people doing it are generally comparable.

To close the pay gap, you raise the pay of the people who are making less so that their pay is in the same general range as the other people doing similar work. There is some room for give and take here.

Look at your salary ranges for the roles. Benchmark what other organizations are paying for similar roles. Then try on solutions and rerun your pay equity analysis to see if it solves the issue.

Affording the Fix

If your budget can't handle closing all the pay gaps for all the people who need it closed, find the best solution you can afford and have a plan and timeline to correct the issues as soon as feasible.

There are two important rules to remember when dealing with pay equity:

- Affordability and budget are not a defense to a discriminatory pay gap.
- You can only raise someone's salary to address pay equity issues; you cannot lower anyone's pay to make things equal.

If your pay equity issue looks bigger than your budget, turn to the friendly employment lawyer who has been guiding you through this and ask for help in crafting the best approach. You need a plan to fix it and do as much as you can as quickly as you can.

Consequences of Pay Inequities

Employees have always talked about pay. And they have a federal right to discuss wages, hours, and working conditions under the National Labor Relations Act. As more states require pay transparency, with some also requiring posting wage ranges in job ads and giving notice to current employees about new internal openings and pay, the information employees have is getting better.

Meanwhile, most employers are going to have some pay equity gaps because wages have been increasing and newer employees are likely to make more money than some longer tenured employees. If you haven't had any issues with pay inequities, it may be tempting to think, "We've made it just fine so far. We don't have problems. Let's wait and see what happens." Here are some of the things that might happen.

Declining Performance and Productivity

The first thing that happens when employees feel that they or their colleagues are being treated unfairly (whether it's true or not) is drama. Word starts circulating that the new guy with less experience is making more than the woman who has been a great performer for five years. People start comparing notes and researching publicly available information about pay at the company and its competitors.

If the culture allows it or if people are brave, employees will start having conversations with their managers about pay and pay equity at the organization. If managers don't have useful information or avoid the discussions, the drama will spill out into social media, Glassdoor reviews, and friends at other organizations.

Drama is distracting. When it seems like one person is being treated unfairly, people start noticing other places where things seem unfair. Then those things become the subject of discussions and research. Lather, rinse, repeat. Absences start to increase as people feel discouraged and some start to look for new jobs. Work doesn't get done well or on time. Then the meetings start about how to get back on track, which is a further distraction.

Unfairness, real or perceived, is corrosive to performance and productivity. And organizations often try to address the productivity issue without considering whether there is an underlying problem. So, if it seems like drama is increasing and performance is decreasing, these are symptoms, not the cause. Find out what's happening and what can be done to address it. For pay equity issues, this usually involves communication, transparency, and money. But let's say the "C'mon team, let's get focused" talk results in some improvement. The next thing that happens is people start leaving.

Turnover

When it's clear to employees that they can make a lot more money if they switch jobs, many will. Often, it's not any more complicated than that—regardless of any pay equity issues.

For some, they don't want to move or change their commute or deal with a new role that isn't exactly what they want to do. For these employees, it takes longer to make the decision to leave. Instead, they will stay, start looking, and wait for the right opportunity. But when employees start to feel and believe that it's not just the market—that there's something else going on and they are being treated unfairly—turnover increases more quickly.

Turnover is always time-consuming, expensive, and a drag on productivity. It's also hard on the people remaining when their team is understaffed and they are working longer for the same pay. When employees miss their colleagues and see that they are happy and making more money elsewhere, turnover can become contagious. In industries with tight labor markets, this can cause disruption to production timelines, service to customers, and even client relationships. Considering all the potential damage to the bottom line, suddenly giving raises to close pay gaps is cost-effective.

Damage to Employer Brand and Recruiting

When people's LinkedIn timelines are filled with connections who have left a specific company and are announcing new jobs, people start to wonder what's wrong. Why are so many people leaving?

Before people apply to openings, they will check in with people who worked there to find out what's going on. If they learn that it's a difficult place to work where there are pay equity issues, they won't apply. No organization can withstand a reputation for treating people unfairly, especially around pay. It's not a place where people will stay or want to work.

Discrimination Claims

Then there are the claims and lawsuits. Pay disparities can violate both pay equity laws and more general employment discrimination laws. The damages can be significant, and if the company loses, it can end up paying both its and the employees' attorney fees.

Even the best employers sometimes get claims. But having to deal with discrimination lawsuits—collecting and producing reams of documents and data, employee depositions, and the additional stress and uncertainty for years sometimes—only makes existing problems worse.

Bottom Line

If a company is really concerned about the bottom line, preventing pay equity issues and closing gaps is an excellent investment and will save you money.

How Unconscious Bias Affects Compensation

Unconscious bias can have a significant impact on compensation within a company. Here are some ways that unconscious bias can affect compensation:

> **Gender Bias**: Research has shown that women are often paid less than men for the same work, even when controlling for factors such as education and experience. Unconscious bias can play a role in this by causing managers to undervalue the work of women or assume that they are less committed to their jobs due to family responsibilities.

Race Bias: Similar to gender bias, unconscious bias can lead to disparities in compensation based on race or ethnicity. Managers may hold stereotypes or assumptions about certain racial groups that can impact their evaluation of an employee's worth or contributions to the company.

Job Evaluation Bias: Unconscious bias can also impact the way that jobs are evaluated and compensated within a company. For example, jobs that are traditionally held by men may be valued higher than jobs that are traditionally held by women, even if the jobs require similar levels of skill or education.

Negotiation Bias: Unconscious bias can impact the negotiation process for salaries and compensation packages. For example, men may be more likely to negotiate for higher salaries, while women may be less likely to do so because of societal expectations or perceptions about gender roles.

Performance Evaluation Bias: Unconscious bias can impact the way that managers evaluate an employee's performance, which can impact their compensation. Managers may hold biases that lead them to evaluate certain employees more positively than others, regardless of their actual performance.

Age Bias: Unconscious bias can lead to age discrimination, where older workers are paid less than younger workers for the same job. This can be due to the perception that older workers are less productive or innovative, which is often untrue.

Appearance Bias: Unconscious bias based on physical appearance can impact compensation, particularly for jobs where appearance is deemed important. For example, attractive people may be paid more or receive better opportunities than less attractive people, even if they have the same qualifications and experience.

Affinity Bias: Unconscious bias can lead to favoritism towards employees who share similar backgrounds or interests with the manager. This can lead to higher compensation or more opportunities for those employees, regardless of their qualifications or performance.

Confirmation Bias: Unconscious bias can lead to confirmation bias, where a manager's pre-existing beliefs about an employee or group of employees influence their compensation decisions. For example, if a manager believes that a particular employee is not as skilled as they actually are, they may unconsciously undervalue their work and compensate them less.

Stereotype Threat: Unconscious bias can lead to stereotype threat, where employees who belong to a stereotyped group (e.g., women, people of color, LGBTQ+ individuals) may underperform because they're afraid of confirming the negative stereotype. This can lead to lower compensation or missed opportunities for advancement.

How to Minimize Unconscious Bias in Compensation

Minimizing bias in compensation is an important step toward creating a more equitable and inclusive workplace. Here are some steps that companies can take to minimize bias in compensation:

Conduct Regular Pay Audits: Companies should conduct regular pay audits to identify and address any pay disparities based on gender, race, or other factors. This can help ensure that compensation decisions are based on objective criteria and are free from bias.

Establish Clear and Transparent Criteria: Companies should establish clear and transparent criteria for compensation decisions. This can include specific job responsibilities, qualifications, and performance metrics. By establishing clear criteria, companies can ensure that compensation decisions are based on objective factors rather than subjective bias.

Provide Training on Unconscious Bias: Companies should provide training on unconscious bias to all managers and employees involved in compensation decisions. This can help raise awareness of unconscious bias and provide tools and strategies to minimize its impact.

Use Anonymous Job Applications and Evaluations: Companies can use anonymous job applications and evaluations to minimize bias in the hiring and compensation process. This can help remove any identifying information that could lead to unconscious bias and ensure that candidates are evaluated solely on their qualifications and experience.

Review Job Descriptions and Requirements: Companies should review job descriptions and requirements to ensure that they are free from bias. This can include removing unnecessary qualifications that may be biased towards certain groups or using gender-neutral language.

Conduct Regular Performance Evaluations: Companies should conduct regular performance evaluations to ensure that compensation decisions are based on objective performance metrics. This can help minimize bias based on personal relationships or affinity bias.

By taking these steps, companies can minimize bias in compensation and create a more equitable and inclusive workplace. It's important for companies to recognize the impact of unconscious bias on compensation and take proactive steps to address it.

CHAPTER 7

Creating a Pay Equity Practice

The key to maintaining pay equity is regular monitoring and advance planning. Monitoring involves keeping your job descriptions, job, and people data up to date and regularly performing a pay equity analysis. You should assess pay equity at least once a quarter and any time there are significant changes in headcount, usually from mergers and acquisitions, layoffs, or pivots involving lots of hiring.

When you know changes in headcount are coming, plan your pay equity audit and budget in advance to close any pay gaps. Then let people know you are doing it. It demonstrates that equity is important to the organization and that you are walking your talk.

Seven Steps to Get Started with a Pay Equity Program

To start a pay equity program, here are the first seven steps to take:

1. **Define the Scope and Goals**: The first step is to define the scope and goals of the pay equity process. This involves identifying the specific job roles and employee groups that will be analyzed, the timeframe for the analysis, and the desired outcome of the process.
2. **Assemble a Team**: Next, assemble a team of stakeholders who will be involved in the pay equity process. This might include

representatives from HR, compensation, legal, and finance departments, as well as employee representatives.

3. **Conduct a Data Inventory**: Collect and inventory all relevant data sources, such as employee data, job descriptions, pay scales, performance metrics, and other related information.

4. **Review Relevant Laws and Regulations**: Review relevant laws and regulations related to pay equity, such as equal pay laws and anti-discrimination laws, to ensure compliance with legal requirements.

5. **Analyze Data for Potential Disparities**: Analyze the data to identify potential disparities in pay, such as pay gaps between male and female employees or between employees of different races or ethnicities.

6. **Evaluate Potential Causes of Disparities**: Once potential disparities are identified, evaluate the potential causes of these disparities. This may involve analyzing job roles, experience levels, education, performance metrics, and other factors that may impact pay.

7. **Develop a Plan of Action**: Based on the analysis and evaluation of the data, develop a plan of action that includes strategies for addressing any pay disparities that were identified. This might include adjusting pay scales, modifying job descriptions, and implementing new policies and procedures to ensure ongoing pay equity.

These first seven steps can help you begin the process of analyzing and addressing pay equity issues and create a roadmap for ongoing pay equity efforts.

How Often to Audit Pay Equity

Auditing pay equity is essential for compliance and important for tracking compensation and equity in your organization. Some states are starting to require reporting and disclosure of the basics of pay equity, including pay ranges and demographics of the people in each of those ranges. For states that have those requirements, reporting is annual.

So the compliance answer is to audit pay equity at least once a year and several months before you have to report so you can fix issues and audit again before you have to report. On a practical level, it's smart to audit pay equity as part of your quarterly reporting. Pay equity should be another people analytics metric that you regularly review to understand where you may have or may soon have pay gaps that could affect your competitiveness in the market. As a practice, audit pay equity as part of your quarterly reporting.

Then there are times when you want to audit because you are going through changes. Mergers, acquisitions, layoffs, or significant hiring events should all have pay equity as part of the process to make sure you won't have compliance issues and to make sure everyone is and will be paid fairly in comparison to everyone else.

The Role of Pay Transparency in Pay Equity

by Sarah Morgan

In the simplest terms, pay transparency is the practice of communicating the pay ranges for specific jobs within an organization, along with the reasoning behind them. In a broader context, pay transparency is the most active and practical component of DEI.

Pay transparency holds organizations accountable to the principles of DEI—policies that promote equal representation of individuals within a workforce, regardless of race, gender, age, sexual orientation, or other factors. When an organization is not only willing to put its money behind its DEI promises but also willing to talk about both pay and pay equity, it's proof they mean it.

Why Pay Transparency Is a Good Thing

Being open about compensation helps everyone. By reviewing and disclosing pay for jobs, employers can see where there may be pay gaps for people doing comparable work and can design a comprehensive pay strategy that helps with consistency and competitiveness across the organization.

For employees, pay transparency helps them understand where they are and where they want to be. Instead of imagining themselves with a title or office, they can see the path and start building the skills and experience they need to get there.

In hiring, candidates know the pay before they apply. They can opt in or out based on whether the pay works for them instead of going through the entire hiring process only to realize they can't take the job. Pay transparency also saves recruiters and hiring managers time because they won't be interviewing people who won't accept an offer. This also saves steps and misunderstandings in negotiating the offer. When you have a reasonable pay range from the start, getting to the right number is much easier and faster.

Disclosing pay from the beginning and making pay transparent to all employees also builds trust and accountability. It's easier to identify issues and address them when the data are available and people are comfortable dealing with it.

Types of Pay Transparency

For some companies, pay transparency may mean disclosure of pay for entire departments or job groups. For others, it may mean full disclosure of pay ranges for every position. Pay transparency can even mean disclosure of the exact salaries of current employees. This level of transparency is required for most government employees.

The ways pay information is shared also varies. For some, salary ranges (either by department or for individual positions) are shared on request. For others, this information is posted and freely available for anyone within the organization to view. Most companies that practice pay transparency fall somewhere in the middle of this range.

How Transparent Do You *Really* Want to Get?

With your pay philosophy in place and your team properly trained, it's time to decide exactly what level of transparency to provide. Beyond the legal mandates, what approach works best for your company? Ask yourself these questions before deciding:

- **How does your pay compare to that of competitors?** How does your compensation stack up when compared to similar positions at other companies? This information is available and, while not always accurate, it can help you can get a good idea of where you stand. You may have to look harder to answer why those numbers are higher or lower than your own.
- **How transparent are your current practices?** What is your current company culture? What information is already available to employees about salaries, job expectations, and performance reviews? What kinds of questions do employees already ask about their pay? Collaborate with HR and any other relevant departments to gain an accurate assessment of your company culture. After reviewing this, you can better determine what kind of culture you'd like to have.
- **What's the worst that could happen?** Consider what could go wrong when implementing pay transparency. Troubleshoot in advance. Determine the potential liabilities at play with your legal team. Consult with department heads to ensure that your desired level of transparency won't complicate any current projects or initiatives. If it will, rethink your approach to all ongoing operations.

Risks and Benefits of Pay Transparency

As you consider pay transparency both from a compliance and a practical perspective, here are the primary risks and benefits of being more transparent about compensations:

- **Risks**
  - Employee dissatisfaction due to perceived unfairness in compensation,
  - Potential legal issues if pay disparities are not addressed, and

    ○ Challenges in managing employee expectations and reactions to pay information.
- **Benefits**
    ○ Improved pay equity and fairness within the organization,
    ○ Enhanced employee trust and satisfaction,
    ○ Attraction and retention of top talent,
    ○ Compliance with relevant laws and regulations, and
    ○ Encouragement of open dialogue about compensation and career growth opportunities.

Using Pay Transparency to Improve Pay Equity

Pay transparency feels awkward for a lot of us. Some of us are uncomfortable talking about money and pay. Some of us think that keeping pay a secret can be a competitive advantage and an important part of managing labor costs. Neither of these things is true. Money is at the heart of the employment relationship. It's what people get in exchange for their work.

The roots of discomfort in talking about money are based in gender discrimination and the history of men controlling property, money, and women. Normalizing pay transparency and discussions about compensation are essential to pay equity and compliance with equal pay and civil rights laws.

As for secrecy, public employees have had their compensation disclosed under open records acts since the 1960s. For everyone else, pay became easy to research online. If you want to know what people typically make in various jobs, industries, and locations, the data are available. While some sources are more reliable than others, pay has not been secret for a very long time. Over a dozen states have passed pay transparency laws that require pay ranges to be disclosed in the hiring process. Some places, like Colorado, California, and New York City, also require the salary range to be included in the job posting.

Disclose Pay in Your Job Posting

Some organizations are trying to comply with pay transparency laws by posting meaningless pay ranges. When the stated pay range is $45,000 to

$125,000, the information isn't useful. Technically, the organization can offer $47,000 because it is in the stated range, but the candidate is probably looking for something over six figures. Everyone's time and energy are wasted.

Overly broad pay ranges also say something about your organization. They say: Yes, we know the rules, but we want to get around them and don't care very much about why they are there. A milder version is: There's this new rule about pay disclosure, but we don't have the time to come up with meaningful pay ranges. We need someone in this role now.

Either way, giving meaningless pay ranges raises red flags for candidates who want to work for organizations that will treat them fairly and whom they can trust. Misleading people in your job ad can do much more damage than you think.

Here's how to effectively post salary ranges:

1. Look at what people in similar roles are making in your organization.
2. Look at the market and what people in comparable roles make.
3. Develop realistic pay ranges based on actual salaries you would offer for the role.
4. Post the applicable salary range.

Yes, it takes some extra thought and work, especially if you don't have complete and accurate pay data. But in long run, it will save you time and money, build trust, and demonstrate fairness. Post the pay.

How to Disclose Pay Internally

Here is a seven-step process for disclosing pay information to employees to increase pay transparency in the organization:

1. **Develop a Pay Transparency Strategy**: Determine the level of pay transparency that aligns with your organization's culture, values, and legal requirements. For example, decide whether to share salary ranges for specific positions or the entire organization.

2. **Conduct an Internal Pay Audit**: Analyze your organization's current compensation practices to identify any pay disparities or inconsistencies.

3. **Address Pay Disparities**: Develop a plan to rectify any identified pay disparities and ensure fair compensation for all employees.

4. **Develop a Pay Philosophy**: Create a clear and consistent pay philosophy that outlines the factors influencing compensation decisions, such as job responsibilities, qualifications, and performance.

5. **Communicate the Pay Structure**: Share the pay structure, including salary ranges and factors influencing pay decisions, with employees and job candidates.

6. **Provide Training and Resources**: Train managers and HR personnel on the pay transparency policy and provide resources to help them communicate effectively with employees about compensation.

7. **Monitor and Adjust**: Regularly review and update the pay transparency policy and process to ensure ongoing compliance, fairness, and effectiveness.

As you move through these questions and consider what level of pay transparency works for your organization, here are some of the common issues, important things to remember, and things to avoid:

- Don't share incomplete or inaccurate pay information.
- Make sure you address pay disparities or inconsistencies.
- Don't ignore legal requirements and regulations related to pay transparency.
- Make sure to encourage open dialogue about compensation.
- Provide appropriate training and resources for managers and HR personnel.

Why Money Is So Hard to Talk About

Some people love talking about money. Most people don't. At best, it often feels impolite. At worst, you may have legal or privacy issues. If any of these issues come up for you, you're not alone.

- **Stigma**: Money is often seen as a taboo topic, and people may feel ashamed or embarrassed to talk about their financial situation. To overcome this issue, it's important to recognize that financial struggles are common and that seeking help is a sign of strength. Talking to a trusted friend, family member, or financial professional can help alleviate feelings of shame or embarrassment.
- **Anxiety and Stress**: Financial stress can lead to anxiety and stress, which can make it difficult to have productive conversations about money. To overcome this issue, it's important to address the underlying causes of financial stress and develop a plan to manage it. This can involve creating a budget, seeking financial counseling, or finding ways to increase income.
- **Different Values and Priorities**: People may have different values and priorities when it comes to money, which can lead to disagreements and conflict. To overcome this issue, it's important to have open and honest conversations about financial goals and priorities. This can involve setting shared financial goals, creating a budget together, and finding ways to compromise.
- **Lack of Knowledge**: Many people lack knowledge about personal finance, which can make it difficult to have informed conversations about money. To overcome this issue, it's important to educate oneself about personal finance. This can involve reading books or articles, attending financial workshops, or seeking advice from a financial professional.
- **Mental Health Issues**: Mental health issues, such as depression or anxiety, can make it difficult to manage money and have

productive conversations about finances. To overcome this issue, it's important to seek professional help for mental health issues. This can involve talking to a therapist or counselor, joining a support group, or seeking medication if necessary.

- **Power Dynamics**: Power dynamics can make it difficult to have productive conversations about money, especially in relationships where one partner has more financial control than the other. To overcome this issue, it's important to have open and honest conversations about financial decision-making and to find ways to share financial control. This can involve creating a joint bank account, setting shared financial goals, and finding ways to compromise.

How to Start Talking about Money

by Trish Steed

Organizations see compensation as a budgeting and business decision. Employees see it differently. For employees, pay is far deeper and more complex than just money for their work. Pay is personal.

When you think about pay, you may have a sense of satisfaction that you are paid what you feel is fair for the time and effort that you provide through your work. If you feel like you are not being paid fairly, it's normal to feel angry, sad, or unappreciated. The feeling of being underpaid can also lead to a high degree of stress.

Emotions around pay can also be incredibly positive. Being paid well and fairly for your work and being recognized for great work through raises and bonuses feels rewarding.

This is part of what makes discussing pay so difficult. But both pay equity and pay transparency depend on the organization's ability to both understand and effectively communicate about pay.

Here's an outline for a training program that helps people have conversations about money. What it looks and sounds like in practice will vary depending on your organization's culture, the resources available, and how transparent you decide to be about compensation.

- **Introduction to Financial Management**: Start with an overview of financial management, including the importance of allocating funds into profitable ventures and making investments that give reasonable returns with safety on the investment made.
- **Internal Pay versus External Benchmarks**: Discuss the challenges of balancing internal pay structures with external benchmarks, and how to navigate these issues in a way that is fair and transparent.
- **Performance Reviews**: Explain how performance reviews can impact pay and how to have constructive conversations about performance and compensation.
- **Asking for a Raise**: Discuss strategies for asking for a raise, including how to prepare for the conversation, how to make a compelling case, and how to negotiate effectively.
- **Turning Down a Request for a Raise**: Address the challenges of turning down a request for a raise and how to do so in a way that is respectful and constructive.
- **Asking for an Advance**: Discuss the pros and cons of asking for an advance and how to have a conversation about this topic with a manager.
- **Granting or Turning Down an Advance**: Explain how to make a decision about granting or turning down an advance and how to communicate this decision in a way that is fair and transparent.
- **Role-Playing Exercises**: Use role-playing exercises to help participants practice having difficult conversations about money and to build their confidence in these situations.
- **Q&A Session**: Allow time for participants to ask questions and share their own experiences, and provide guidance and feedback as needed.

- **Follow-Up Resources**: Provide participants with additional resources, such as articles, books, or online courses, that can help them continue to build their skills and knowledge around financial management and having conversations about money.

Managing Wage Compression and Pay Equity

Pay equity is about making sure people doing comparable work are paid equally. For pay equity, any differences in pay must be based on legitimate business reasons and not based on gender, race, or other protected factors.

Wage compression is when the pay range for similar work becomes narrower and people with less experience or tenure sometimes are paid higher than people with more tenure and experience. It usually happens when wages for new hires are increasing and wages for existing employees stay the same.

Addressing pay equity can push compensation toward being the same; addressing wage compression can push compensation to be different. It's a little like two dogs tugging on the same stick. And it's easy to get off balance. The goal is to find the sweet spot and a pay range that fairly compensates everyone while considering the work they do and the differences that justify higher pay in specific cases.

Under equal pay laws, you can pay people differently if the skills, effort, and responsibilities involved in the work justify the pay differences. If the work is similar, then differences in pay can generally be based on seniority; a merit system; a pay system based on quantity or quality of output; or any factor other than gender, race, or other protected class. This includes differences in geography and cost of living, performance, experience, and skills. Basically, there has to be a good business reason why one person makes more than another.

Finding the Right Salary Range Based on Internal and Market Factors

You want a salary range that is wide enough to avoid wage compression and gives you room to pay people more or less based on legitimate factors. But you also can't make the pay range so wide that it becomes meaningless.

Overly wide pay ranges make it hard to assess pay equity. If you have people at the top and the bottom of a wide pay range doing comparable work, it becomes difficult to justify the pay differentials.

To find the right pay ranges, you need data. Start with your internal pay ranges and compare those to tenure. Are you seeing newer employees making almost as much as or more than longer term employees? If so, you want to check market data and benchmark against what's happening for similar jobs in your industry and, if people work on site, geographic areas.

What you want are competitive wages for newer people and people you don't want to leave for higher pay. You also need room for pay increases as employees gain experience and tenure at the same level. This is different from pay increases for promotions to a different job level.

This is going to look different at every organization, and there's no secret recipe. For example, if people usually stay in one level for two to three years, you can have a narrower pay range than if they stay at the same level for five to six years. If you are seeing wage compression, then look at broadening your pay range and giving increases to employees who are under market rates.

If your budget does not support raises for lots of people, think about what can make a difference so that people want to come and stay even though they can make more money somewhere else. Flexible schedules, a four-day workweek, remote work, or more time off are all important to employees and can have less effect on productivity than you might expect.[1]

Monitoring Pay Equity

To make sure that any adjustments are also consistent with pay equity, it's important to run a pay equity analysis every time you make significant changes to compensation or the work people are doing. You should also audit pay equity at least every quarter no matter what.

Pay equity analysis tools will show you where people are on the salary range for that group of comparable jobs and identify outliers—people at the low and high ends—and whether there are pay gaps that are correlated to gender or race. (Some tools allow analysis of other demographic factors as well.) Once you identify pay gaps that may be related to gender or race, then you look at whether the differences in pay are related to legitimate business factors or whether they may be the result of bias.

Your pay equity solution should also allow you to try out different options to close pay gaps and see how adjusting one person's pay affects pay equity in that group of jobs. To address pay equity, you can only raise some-one's pay. You can't lower it.

By monitoring wage compression, pay equity, and the market and under-standing why you pay people what you do, you can stay in compliance and maintain a competitive pay structure to recruit and retain the people you need.

How Merit Increases Affect Pay Equity

Merit increases can affect pay equity in various ways. Here are some of the ways and proposed solutions to each problem.

High and Low Performers

Merit increases can widen the pay gap between high and low perform-ers. If high performers receive a higher merit increase than low performers, it can lead to pay inequity. To solve this problem, you can establish a merit matrix that considers both performance and pay equity. A merit matrix is a two-factored table that helps equitably allocate raises across their employee population.

It provides a framework for managers and guides them through the merit increase decision-making process. A merit matrix should include the following:

- Distribution of employees across the matrix,
- Merit factors to be used in the matrix based on how merit pay is awarded,
- Pay range spread for each factor, and
- Amount of merit increase for each employee.

Underrepresented Groups

Merit increases can perpetuate pay inequity for underrepresented groups. If underrepresented groups are already paid less than their counterparts, a merit increase based on their current salary can perpetuate the pay gap.

To solve this problem, you can use a compa-ratio, which compares an employee's salary to the midpoint of the salary range for their position. If an employee's compa-ratio is below one, it means they are paid below the midpoint and may need a higher merit increase to achieve pay equity. Companies can also move employees from their current pay to their new role's range low. If this is less than 7 percent, they can give them more to increase pay equity.

Employees in the Same Position

Merit increases can perpetuate pay inequity for employees in the same role. If employees in the same role are already paid differently, a merit increase based on their current salary can perpetuate the pay gap. To solve this problem, companies can establish a merit matrix that considers both performance and pay equity.

CHAPTER 8

Looking Forward: Pay Equity and the Future

There will be more competition for workers as the US labor shortage continues. This will make recruiting and retention essential. In the meantime, technology, approaches to hiring, and how we see and value people's work are all changing. Each of these makes pay equity an important component of finding, keeping, and developing people for the challenges coming.

The Labor Shortage and Pay Equity

by John Sumser

We have a labor shortage that is not going away any time soon. It's been coming for a long time as the baby boomers retire, people are having fewer children, and immigration has tightened.

Why Is This in a Pay Equity Book?

You might be surprised to see a chapter on the labor shortage in this pay equity book. It seems like the topic blossomed overnight as a part of the pandemic. You're about to learn why a pay equity program is the foundation of effective competition for employees in the years to come. Pay equity simultaneously strengthens your ability to compete, solidifies and grounds the national economy, and helps build effective solutions to growing shortages.

Twenty-five years ago, McKinsey published a report called *The War for Talent*[1] in their quarterly magazine. In the years since, all sorts of employment practices were rationalized by the fear of labor shortages that never seemed to materialize. From a practical perspective, the problem never felt real.

Google Trends reports that interest in the topic roared in the early part of the century (see Figure 8.1). It became less of a concern as time marched on.[2] Until the pandemic, talk of heavy competition for workers was relegated to the posturing of HR technology companies looking for market traction.

The underlying story in McKinsey's report was that the problem would emerge from a combination of factors, including the demands of economic growth, an aging population, a mismatch between college output and business needs, changed immigration policies, and a continued migration of the educated to coastal cities.

Concerns about a labor shortage had an inverse trajectory according to Google (see Figure 8.2).[3] While there was some overlapping interest in the early 2000s, interest peaked as the pandemic took root.

Yes, we all knew about the growing shortage of healthcare workers. Skilled tradespeople experienced extraordinary wage growth driven by

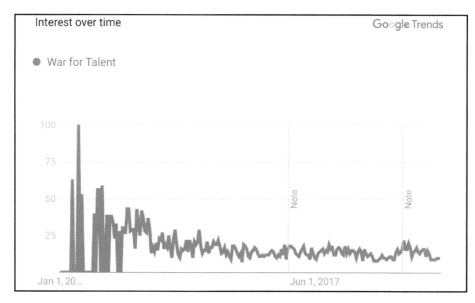

Figure 8.1. Google Trends: War for Talent

labor supply shortages. And as the manufacturing industry moved offshore, there were often concerns about the depletion of our knowledge base. But we didn't see restaurant closings, curtailed retail hours, or wage increases at fast food restaurants until just now.

What Happened and Why Are Things Different?

At the heart of the original War for Talent were two demographic certainties. First, family size (the number of children in a family) continues to be in a decades-long decline. Tightly coupled with the availability of birth control, tough choices between family and career for women, and the economic necessity of two-wage-earner families, birthrates have declined from the post–World War II fertility high of 3.5 babies per woman to the current 1.8. Although babies do not come in fractions, we are producing half of the children we did two generations ago, both by choice and necessity. Figure 8.3 shows the dramatic fall-off in births.[4] Things got worse in the pandemic.

The second demographic certainly is a result of the first. Fewer children means fewer workers down the line. As a result, the average age of the

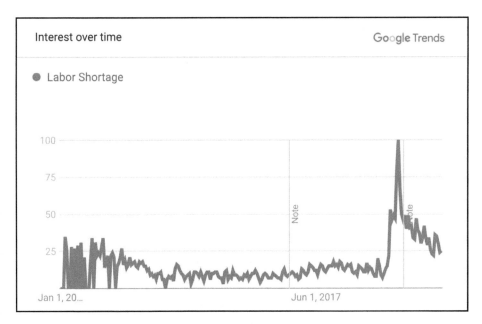

Figure 8.2. Google Trends: Labor Shortage

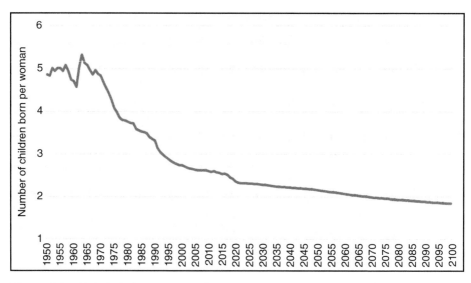

Figure 8.3. Global Birthrates Over Time (*Source*: UN Department of Economic and Social Affairs)

workforce is increasing. As each year passes, more people retire than enter the workforce. So the number of available workers is in an inevitable state of permanent decline.

That's the heart of the reason that labor shortages, in the form of steeper competition, were expected to emerge. Continued economic growth collided with shrinking family size and the aging of the population.

The unemployment rate has fallen since 2009 with a short-lived spike due to COVID-19 shutdowns in 2020 (see Figure 8.4).[5] Below 4 percent, unemployment sits at historic lows, last seen in the late 1960s and the early 1950s.

Meanwhile, economic growth was solid and consistent for a dozen years, which created demand for more workers.

The number of immigrants in the workforce when compared to the overall population has shifted. In 1990, immigrants were 7.9 percent of the US population. In 2020, they were 13.7 percent of the population. In 2021, the US Census Bureau estimated that most immigrant workers in the US (65 percent) worked in five major industry groupings:

- Educational services, healthcare, and social assistance (20.4 percent),
- Professional, scientific, management, administrative, and waste management services (14.5 percent),

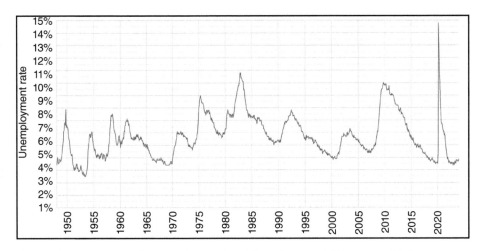

Figure 8.4. US Unemployment Rates Over Time (*Source*: US Bureau of Labor Statistics)

- Manufacturing (11 percent),
- Construction (9.9 percent), and
- Arts, entertainment, recreation, accommodation, and food services (8.8 percent).[6]

But immigrants as the percentage of the workforce has increased substantially. In 1990, immigrants made up 9.2 percent of the US workforce. Foreign-born workers now account for over 17 percent of the workforce.[7] This is almost twice the percentage from 1990. Going from one in ten to nearly one in five happened gradually, then all at once. Today's workforce is significantly more diverse than it was twenty-five years ago. This increased US reliance on foreign-born workers was also significant in the dramatic political shifts of the mid-2010s, especially on the right, to limit immigration.

What Happened in the Pandemic?

Like it or not, believe it or not, we are in a permanent labor shortage. While birth rates fell, the population aged, the economy grew, and immigration contracted, the impact on the workforce grew slowly. It took the COVID-19 pandemic to alert us to the change. Although the demographic forecasts were correct, the effect was never abrupt. A slow decline can be both imperceptible and terribly disruptive.

It's like the game Jenga, where players take turns removing one block at a time from a tower constructed of fifty-four blocks. Each block removed is then placed on top of the tower, creating a progressively more unstable structure. Eventually, one player tugs out a block and the tower crashes.

While our economic Jenga tower won't ever crash completely, the metaphor is instructive. When COVID-19 hit, the unemployment rate rose overnight to about 15 percent. More than 10 percent of the workforce lost their jobs in an instant. In late 2022, the US Chamber of Commerce reported that while job openings have increased steadily since 2020, there are three million more workers not participating in the labor force compared to February 2020.[8]

The US Chamber of Commerce surveyed people who had not returned to the workforce. Over half were either ill themselves or taking care of someone else:

- Illness or disability (28 percent)
- Taking care of children or someone disabled or ill (27 percent)[9]

COVID-19 shook our conventional definitions of what was work and who was essential. We learned to think carefully about where work was done and why. We grasped the health hazards that accompany public-facing jobs. And suddenly many people were working in new ways and places because our children were home and so were we.

Here are some of the key issues revealed by the COVID-19 shutdown:

- **Childcare**: Many parents, mostly women, left the labor force to care for their children during the time of remote schooling. They discovered that there is only a marginal difference in income when you don't pay for childcare, commutes, professional wardrobe, eating out, and an increased tax bill. As a result, these people are not returning to the workforce.
- **Importance of Undocumented Workers**: The combination of increased surveillance of undocumented workers and heightened

health risks drove formerly employed workers further into the gray labor market and out of service jobs. Eighty-one percent of restaurant operators say they are short at least one position. Servers and dishwashers are in the highest demand, and one-third of restaurants report that they are short on both positions.

- **Declining Workforce Participation**: By late 2022, the workforce participation rate continued to fall by about 0.1 percent each month. That means 160,000 fewer workers each month. The decline has been going on for decades because of many factors including an aging workforce, women becoming the majority of college students and degree earners, and the deaths and long-term health issues because of COVID-19.

- **Senior Caretaking**: The aging population requires a constantly increasing supply of assistants to care for the elderly and infirm. In the absence of a dependable supply of undocumented help, workers must leave the workforce to meet these family obligations.

- **Mismatched Expectations**: There is a group of workers aged between 22 and 35 with college educations who remain on the economic sidelines. The labor shortages are largely in areas that require no education and have low economic status. These potential workers are burdened with educational debt and can't afford to live on lower-wage jobs.

- **Accelerated Retirement**: About three million workers, of retirement age, were prompted by COVID-19 to begin their retirements. The newly retired were senior people with enough resources to retire. They were middle- and senior-level people with extensive career track records. They helped us see that the slow departure of the baby boomer generation had been ongoing and was now accelerating. The acceleration is driven by age, not fundamental economics.

- **Productivity Increases**: Indicators for productivity were stubbornly flat for the decade preceding COVID-19. Remote work and expanded workplace flexibility turned out to be powerful ways to increase worker output. Many chose to stay remote and learned to work as independent contractors.

- **Healthcare and Teacher Shortages Multiplied**: Generally underpaid and overstressed, both healthcare and education workers faced (and continue to face) serious health risks. Attrition in these professions hit new highs.

COVID-19 didn't cause the labor shortage. Rather, it opened our eyes to existing issues while accelerating the trends that were coming anyway.

Where Are the Shortages?

The primary labor shortfalls are in lower-wage industries that have lost workers to higher paying jobs in construction, warehousing, and professional and business services. As of late 2022, the *Washington Post* reported that the following industries were still missing significant numbers of workers from before the pandemic:

- Hospitality and leisure industry were down 1.2 million workers.
- Public schools were missing almost 360,000 workers.
- Healthcare has lost 37,000 workers.
- Rail transportation was down 12,500 workers.[10]

Meanwhile, people working are exhausted, burnt out, and considering other options. The American Psychological Association's 2021 Work and Well-Being Survey of US workers showed that 79 percent of employees had experienced work-related stress in the previous month. Some of the specifics included the following:

- 19 percent felt diminished effort at work;
- 26 percent experienced disinterest, low motivation, or low energy;
- 32 percent were emotionally exhausted;
- 36 percent had cognitive weariness; and
- 44 percent reported physical fatigue—a 38 percent increase since 2019.[11]

This is neither sustainable nor improving.

Is the Labor Shortage Permanent?

The short answer is yes, the labor shortage is permanent. Five factors guarantee a continued shrinkage of the workforce:

- **Low Immigration**: Continued immigration restrictions will cause increasing labor shortages in jobs that do not require higher education.
- **Family Size and Fertility**: Many workers considering families are the same people who can't afford childcare, have concerns about the future and climate change, and are uncomfortable with the current political climate that has sought to limit women's rights and autonomy. There are also indications that COVID-19 affects fertility, which could further diminish population.
- **Workforce Participation**: The tail end of the baby boomers will likely be retiring in the next decade, and there are not enough workers to replace them all. Meanwhile we are waiting to understand the effects of long COVID-19 on both worker participation and the need for caregivers.
- **Aging Population**: As people retire, the percentage of people not working will continue to increase, putting additional stresses on healthcare and elder care.
- **Economic Growth**: Even with advances in technology and automation, the economy cannot continue to grow with sustained labor shortages. A continued lack of workers could disrupt many of our economic systems that are based on continuous growth.

Possible Solutions

To solve a labor shortage, you can either increase the number of workers or decrease the number of jobs. The only other options are offshoring work and increasing immigration. We may see more of the former, although many countries are experiencing similar labor shortages. And eventually, we will have to address immigration as well. In the meantime, attraction and retention will be essential for the foreseeable future.

Attraction means either competing more fiercely for the limited talent available or rethinking the requirements for the job. When employers begin poaching people from the competition, increasing wages, or both, this does not actually increase the number of workers. Rethinking of the job can range from looking more broadly for candidates to reimagining the skill levels and requirements.

Why not both? Employers who are willing to both find and develop people expand their access to the labor pool while making their operation a more attractive place to work.

Last, pay equity will be an important element of hiring and retaining employees. We will have an increasingly diverse workforce, including disability, neurodiversity, age, and backgrounds. Many of our workers have experienced discrimination based on who they are. Providing an inclusive workplace and equitable pay will be essential to retaining workers.

Pay Equity Is Critical for Talent Acquisition

by Madeline Laurano

Talent acquisition has become more complex over the past few years. The labor shortage, pandemic, and uncertain economy have shifted the relationship between candidate and employer. Candidates expect more transparency from the recruitment process, and companies must offer fair and equitable experiences, including information on how employees are paid. As a result, pay equity is a critical part of the future of talent acquisition and an essential component of overcoming discrimination in the workplace.

Pay equity is also a powerful employer branding tool and helps companies attract talent and differentiate themselves in a competitive job market. Candidates are demanding salary disclosures around equity early in the process, and recently enacted laws in several states are requiring companies to provide more transparency to job seekers. But as the conversations around pay equity accelerate, most companies lack the strategies or technology to support change, and the tight labor market has put some companies at risk if they are not running pay analysis or investing in the right solutions. For pay equity to be part of a talent acquisition strategy, employers must rethink their current processes and technology.

The Current State of Talent Acquisition

Talent acquisition is in a state of transformation. Some companies have accelerated hiring to meet the demands of the business, while others have shifted their hiring goals. According to Aptitude Research, 92 percent of companies are still hiring even if their focus has changed. And while different regions and sectors face many challenges in recruiting talent, every organization is transforming, and talent acquisition leaders are uniquely positioned to help influence this change.

Humanity Is a Critical Part of Strategic Talent Acquisition

Companies must carefully consider the experiences of both recruiters and candidates. Recruiters are overworked and looking for new opportunities, and candidates are not receiving fair and equitable experiences. The future of talent acquisition includes improved experiences and more trust around the recruitment process.

This focus on humanity places new responsibilities on talent acquisition including an increased focus on pay equity. But, as the talent acquisition function grows in scale, it also grows in complexity, and executing on these strategies is challenging. By adding new roles, strategies, and technology in a short time, talent acquisition at many companies is unwieldy and difficult to manage. Shifts in recruitment models, levels of responsibility, and experiences are influencing discussions around pay equity and strategic talent acquisition.

Shifts in Recruitment Models

Before and during the pandemic, nearly half of companies surveyed stated that they had a centralized recruitment model. In 2022, 60 percent of companies had shifted to centralized recruitment. According to Aptitude Research, 69 percent of high-performing companies have a centralized model. Centralized recruiting can benefit a company by offering standard processes and consistent strategies throughout the organization. In addition, it can provide a framework for recruiters and accountability through the hiring process.

Although there are numerous advantages of a centralized recruitment model, it also presents challenges as it relates to pay equity. For example, a centralized recruitment model can make it more difficult to respond to local needs for geographically dispersed organizations with multiple offices. Also, a centralized recruitment model can be challenging during times of change when it can slow down the process instead of providing a flexible or transparent response. As companies look at embracing pay equity, they must consider how their current recruitment model (see Figure 8.5) can help or hurt these initiatives.

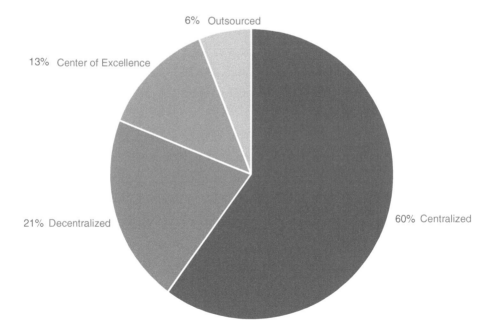

Figure 8.5. Recruitment Models (*Source*: Aptitude Research)

Shifts in Ownership

Talent acquisition is no longer operating in a silo. Instead, every part of the business is directly impacted by the organization's ability to find and attract talent. As a result, companies see more involvement and collaboration from other areas of HR and leadership in talent acquisition activities. The role of talent acquisition professionals is also changing to meet different expectations from these stakeholders (see Figure 8.6). Talent management, learning and development, chief HR officers, and leadership all contribute to talent acquisition strategies.

Surprisingly, only 42 percent of companies state that the chief diversity officer is involved in talent acquisition decisions, even though over 90 percent state that reducing bias is a top priority. For pay equity to be a priority in talent acquisition, companies must consider greater collaboration across key stakeholders and include DEI leaders in both strategy and execution of hiring goals.

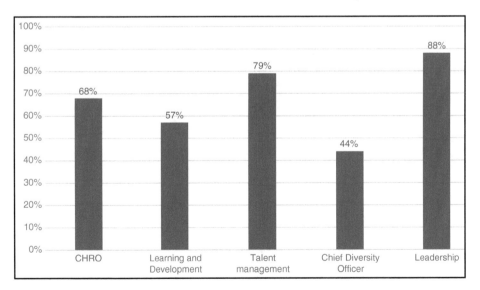

Figure 8.6. Key Stakeholder Involvement in Talent Acquisition (*Source*: Aptitude Research)

Challenges with Pay Equity

Pay equity is complicated, and talent acquisition professionals face several challenges when trying to address it:

- **Getting Leadership Support**: Although most leaders support fairness and equality in the workforce, not every leader supports an equal pay philosophy. Lack of leadership support can negatively impact talent acquisition's commitment to improve pay equity in the hiring process.

- **Lack of Pay Information in the Job Description**: Companies invest in improving the language of job descriptions to ensure fairness but often leave out information on pay. Candidates are left uninformed and misguided as they go through the screening, interview, and assessment process. The lack of transparency in the job description impacts the ability for companies to recruit top talent.

- **Lack of Equal Pay Analysis**: Companies cannot address pay equity in talent acquisition until they understand their pay gaps. A pay equity analysis can help companies to better understand what they need to improve.

- **Tight Labor Market**: An ongoing competitive labor market has made it challenging for companies to attract and recruit talent. In a labor shortage, market conditions influence speed and the need to improve efficiency. Companies looking to hire quickly often ignore critical aspects of pay equity including running pay gap analysis.

Candidate Experience and Pay Equity

Transparency matters. Companies must be transparent about their employer brand, financial performance, and pay. In addition, recruiters must be transparent about the candidate's experience, career development, and company culture. While this level of transparency is positive and can ensure better quality of hires, it adds an extra layer of complexity. Talent Board found five consistent hallmarks of an excellent candidate experience:

1. **Communication**: Communication should be transparent and consistent around pay.
   Business Impact: If communication with a candidate is strong, it reflects positively on the employer brand and impacts the customer experience.

2. **Expectations**: Companies must set realistic expectations for pay and what is coming next in the process.
   Business Impact: If expectations are met, companies build trust and loyalty with candidates that will translate to customer retention and referrals.

3. **Feedback**: Incorporating feedback opportunities makes the process more engaging and personal. The feedback candidates give may be negative, but it increases their positive impressions. On the flip side, providing feedback to final-stage candidates is also essential because it will let them know why they did not move forward.
   Business Impact: If candidates receive feedback, they are more likely to stay loyal to a brand and share their experience with friends and family.

4. **Transparency**: The more transparent and accountable employers are with candidates, the better their experience will be and the more they will trust an employer.
   Business Impact: If a company provides transparency, candidates are more likely to stay engaged and employers are less likely to lose quality talent.

5. **Fairness**: Candidates that are accepted and rejected should leave feeling like they were treated fairly and equitable in the decision-making process.
   Business Impact: If companies provide a fair, equitable, and inclusive experience, they are more likely to improve diverse hiring efforts.

Pay equity directly impacts each of these pillars, and evaluating and monitoring pay equity promotes each of these aspects of recruiting. According to Talent Board, candidate experience is negatively impacted when time is disrespected, the process takes too long, and the salary does not meet expectations. These are the primary reasons why candidates withdraw from the recruiting process (see Figure 8.7).

At a basic level, candidates want to be treated like humans. In the consumer world, if a customer orders something, they expect to receive communication on when it will be delivered or if it is unavailable. In talent acquisition, candidates often receive little information or insights around pay. It is not included in many job descriptions or postings, and companies are hesitant to share this information. Candidates deserve to be treated with respect and fairness and not have to wait until the offer to learn how much a job pays. When these basic requirements are not met, it is nearly impossible to gain trust.

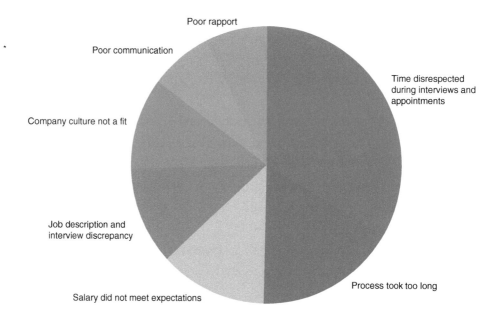

Figure 8.7. Negative Reasons Why Candidates Withdraw from the Recruiting Process (*Source*: Talent Board)

Pay Equity and High-Volume Hiring

High-volume recruitment is the practice of filling many positions in a short time. It encompasses more than hourly or gig workers and includes industries such as aerospace and defense, technology, and financial services. Companies must find quality talent while managing hundreds, or even thousands, of applicants.

Unlike traditional corporate hiring, high-volume needs are extremely time-sensitive and speed is the measure of success. In 2022, high-volume hiring intensified as many companies tried to reduce time-to-fill from several weeks to several days. Unfortunately, the result was often both time-consuming and ineffective.

Pay equity is not a new topic in high-volume recruitment, but it is one that plays a major role in decision-making. According to Aptitude Research, 70 percent of companies believe they are losing talent because of pay transparency and inequities. Companies with low hourly rates or that do not offer competitive rates will lose candidates in the process.

Aptitude Research found that 44 percent of candidates that drop out of the process do so when they find out the pay for a position, and only 30 percent of candidates learn about pay during the application stage (see Figure 8.8). Offering more pay transparency earlier in the high-volume hiring process will save both candidates and companies time and resources.

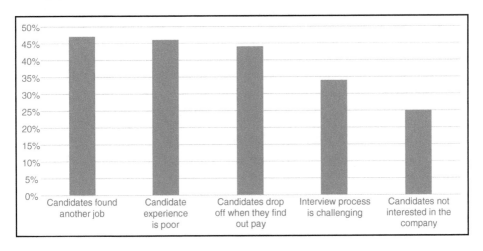

Figure 8.8. Reasons That High-Volume Candidates Drop Out (*Source*: Aptitude Research)

Key Strategies to Improve Pay Equity in Recruiting

To improve both pay equity and the overall hiring process, companies should consider these key strategies:

- **Eliminate Salary Negotiations**: Salary negotiations and the strategies to successfully negotiate are not often available or taught to candidates, especially those starting their careers. As a result, salary negotiations exacerbate the pay gap for minority employees and the effect goes beyond the talent acquisition phase. Not only do salary negotiations place undue stress on candidates to navigate these contentious conversations (and potentially lose income); they also often result in the perpetuation of internal pay inequities among their employees.

- **Invest in the Right Technology Partner**: Talent acquisition is on the front line of pay equity. Tech solutions should provide talent acquisition leaders with the tools they need to determine compensation, include pay transparency, convert quality applicants to hires, and improve the new hire experience. As talent acquisition evolves, recruiters need flexible solutions to support candidates and employers. New tech should allow talent acquisition leaders and recruiters to combine data with authenticity to see offer history, analyze compensation data, and create compelling offers built on transparency and trust.

- **Conduct Pay Equity Assessments**: Companies must regularly conduct pay equity analysis to help to close the pay gap. Pay gap analysis can help provide visibility into what needs to be improved in a company's efforts to address pay equity.

- **Include Pay in Job Descriptions**: Companies that provide pay transparency in job descriptions attract more talent and improve the trust between candidates and employers. By including pay information, candidates have a clear idea of what to expect during the job process and if they will be compensated fairly.

How Technology Is Changing Compensation Practices and Pay Equity

by George LaRocque

While determining compensation has always been part of work, the addition of data, computing, and technology has changed how we determine and manage compensation. It's also made addressing pay equity faster and easier.

There are three market drivers for adopting and investing in HR technology and pay equity is part of each of them:

- **Compliance**: *Rules, standards, policies, requirements, regulations, laws, and transparency.*

   Compliance is the necessity that created the market for HR technology. The need to hire and pay employees while being compliant with laws and regulations makes payroll technology and services a must-have for employers of all sizes.

   Pay equity is a compliance issue in the US, where the Equal Pay Act of 1963 prohibits wage discrimination based on sex and forty-two states have enacted equal pay regulations or laws. Most other countries also have some form of regulation regarding fair and equal pay. Compliance alone motivates innovators to develop tech solutions and businesses to buy them, delivering the "must-have" versus the "nice to have."

- **Experience**: *Technology, goals, innovation, and performance.*

   Experience is the driver of tech adoption. Technology delivering an experience fitting seamlessly into the flow of work results in more people using a product while delivering more data for business insights and improving the users' lives. Some say we're living in an "experience economy."

- **Impact**: *Environmental, social, and governance (ESG) standards; company culture; HR key performance indicators (KPIs); and business impact.* Impact is the metric that the business ties to its business decision. This measurement may be traditional KPIs or the return on investment (ROI) delivered by the tech. Increasingly, impact is tied to technology's role in delivering on the company's mission, vision, values, and culture. As more businesses look at incorporating ESG commitments in their public-facing statements, impact is driving more technology investments and buying decisions.

WorkTech has tracked investment data flowing into the HR technology market since January 2017. HR technology investments are tracked across fifty-three categories, spanning the entire HR lifecycle. Although pay equity is not a stand-alone category, data supporting strategies, workflows, and tactics that impact pay equity appear in six primary categories:

- **Compensation**: Technologies providing capabilities and data focused strictly on compensation.
- **Analytics**: Stand-alone analytics products that are focused on HR metrics
- **Payroll**: Payroll systems.
- **Core HR**: Traditional HRIS systems that act as the "system of record" for employee-centric data.
- **HR Suites/Platforms**: HR platforms that cross over two or more categories in the HR technology ecosystem.
- **Diversity, Equity, and Inclusion (DEI)**: Applications focused on measuring, monitoring, and improving diversity, equity, and inclusion.

Starting in January 2017 and ending in early Q4 2022, $10.8 billion across 260 investments were made in these categories (see Figure 8.9).

Trends Driving Investment and Adoption

While the data measuring investment and adoption of technology focused on pay equity and compensation show a consistent increase, our qualitative research gives us a glimpse of why this is happening.

The shift from HR technology to work technology. As companies continue to drive business and digital transformation against a societal backdrop requiring more transparency, legacy HR and HR technology models are being cast aside for new processes. These new approaches are more inclusive of the entire enterprise. The data captured in these processes are more fluid, and transparency is expected at every level. Top-down "command and control" approaches to processes or technology are not acceptable in the new future of work—more than just a new name for HR technology—work tech is the emerging technology category representing people issues in the flow of work.

Talent is the core of every business. Forty-seven percent of CEOs that WorkTech surveyed feel that talent-related concerns are their most critical business problems. Perhaps nothing embodies this focus more than the emerging trend in "talent intelligence," which draws data and insights from external labor market data, core HR and talent systems data, and data across

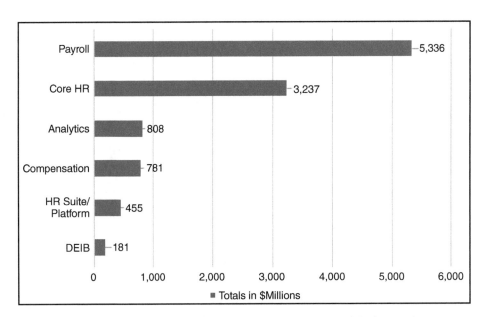

Figure 8.9. Investments in HR Tech (2017–2020) (*Source*: WorkTech ongoing research, www.1.worktech.com)

the enterprise to support strategic business decisions. Compensation data is inherent in all talent intelligence elements and its supporting tech stack.

Compensation and offer data as market intelligence. Another shift we've discovered in our research is the emergence of leveraging compensation data to both make more competitive offers and ensure pay equity and transparency. Through a combination of traditional salary survey data, compensation data captured through the hiring process, and anonymous compensation data shared by employers through a shared tech vendor or data provider, employers can make new hire and internal compensation offers that are more competitive at the time of offer. The recency of the data used ensures this. When this process is integrated with rules and practices put in place by compensation and total rewards teams, it ensures both compliance and pay equity.

Skills, Opportunities, and Equity at Work

by Steve Boese

While pay equity can be researched, assessed, and acted on in any organization, it is only part of a broader set of human capital management and talent challenges facing organizations today. And certainly, the wider set of challenges look and feel different from just a few years ago, as the global pandemic altered almost every organization, brought new problems, made others less important, and raised the importance of still others.

At the end of the last decade, many organizations were primarily concerned with the "skills gap"—that jobs and the skills required to do them were changing. In many cases, the change was happening more rapidly than the people in the organization could adapt. Organizations found themselves challenged to find workers with these skills in the labor market. Part of the skills gap discussion was the debate over automation of work and the potential displacement of workers by new technologies like artificial intelligence (AI), robotic process automation, and advanced machinery. Work was changing more quickly than HR leaders and employees were prepared for. And both HR leaders and individual employees were faced with determining the best strategies for navigating the workplace of the future. But it was becoming clearer that new skills were going to be needed and acquiring them was the most important challenge coming into 2020.

With the skills conversation, people began to realize that a focus on skills instead of experience or education could expand opportunities and have a democratizing effect on the workplace. If the organization could select people for jobs based on skills and could compensate people based on the acquisition and exercise of these skills in a fair way, that would make organizations much more agile and resilient.

The Pivot to Skills-Based Talent Management

This realization by organizational leaders, researchers, and HR leaders that skills were the currency of the new workforce has led to new ideas on how work was to be organized. Jobs did not need to be narrowly defined and people no longer had to fit specific jobs. Instead, organizations and HR leaders could determine the specific skills needed for the work, then match people having the needed skills to those tasks, projects, and teams.

In this new approach, skills, rather than formal degrees, would be used in hiring decisions. Workforce planning would compare the skills the organization requires compared to the skills possessed by the workforce to make plans and budgets. And importantly, compensation and rewards would have to be reimagined and updated to reflect a skills-centered model.

This has led to structured methodologies for analyzing jobs and deconstructing them into collections of tasks. From tasks, we can determine the specific skills needed for that work. Then we can evaluate workers' skills based on their past and current work. This allows organizations to map the work to skills and determine the best approach to getting it done.

Let's give an example of how that might look for a sample job. Claims processing is a common job for insurers. This role would include tasks like assessing the nature of the claim and coverage under the policy, negotiating claims payments, processing settlements, and recommending new procedures and policies. Next, a workforce planner would estimate the percentage of time devoted to each task and the cost/budget for the overall role. From there, the nature of each task is evaluated to determine the types of skills that are needed for the work, such as the following:

- Is the task repetitive in nature or variable?
- Does the worker perform the task independently or more collaboratively with colleagues?
- Does the task require specific physical attributes or capabilities to complete or is it mainly mental in nature?

Then the planner can look at whether the tasks can be performed by automation, outsourcing, or even eliminating the tasks entirely.

More nuanced analysis may determine that the human worker should still be responsible for performing the tasks but certain parts can be augmented by technology to make completion faster or more accurate. The organization may find that 25 percent of the tasks of claims processing roles can be automated, opening the possibility of redesigning the job. The insurer may decide that claims processors should spend more time working with the insureds or investigating the claim. Thus, the claims processors develop more proficiency in the kinds of skills that have more long-term value to the organization and for their own career development.

The concerns about automation, robotics, and artificial intelligence leading to widespread displacement of workers have seemed to pause, as pandemic-era concerns, extended remote working arrangements, and macroeconomic concerns have dominated the discourse about the workplace. But the new work model of framing the organization as a collective of skills and capabilities, and its workforce as flexible, developing, and providers of value through their skills, is a positive step towards more equitable opportunities and outcomes.

Skills and Compensation

If we approach work as a collection of skills instead of a collection of jobs, then how do we determine compensation? For organizations that use the jobs to classify workers and organize work, employees could have both a base salary based on the traditional compensation range assigned to that job and a "skills" salary component that is calculated from the market value of the skills and the current organizational demand for these skills. This blended approach to compensation would enable people to be rewarded in line with market demand for their skills, which can fluctuate over time, while allowing the organization to still retain basic job structures.

There are two clear benefits to this approach. First, with broader job classifications, it becomes easier for employees to move to new opportunities within the organization, as internal mobility will be less restrained by narrow job definitions. And second, employees should see improved fairness and access to internal opportunities, as focus moves from job definitions and more towards the specific skills needed and the skills that people possess, regardless of whether they are in the "right" position in a traditional organizational chart.

An alternative would be to make compensation completely based on an individual's bundle of skills, pegged to the market value of these skills and the organization's current and expected future requirements. Even if compensation is only partially based on discrete skills, workers and leaders alike see this transition to more skills-based compensation in a positive light. According to a report from Deloitte titled *Building Tomorrow's Skills-Based Organization: Jobs Aren't Working Anymore*, 74 percent of workers are in favor of moving toward skills-based pay and transparency, as are 78 percent of business leaders.[12]

For as long as employees have been surveyed about their plans to remain or stay in their current jobs, there have been two primary factors that influence an employee's decision process: money and opportunity to grow and advance. Total compensation is usually the number one driver of career mobility decision-making. Number two is "career development," "skills development," and/or "opportunities for advancement." A study published by Pew Research Center in March 2022 asked workers who quit their jobs in 2021 why they left. The top reasons were the same—compensation and lack of opportunities for advancement, both cited by 63 percent of respondents.[13]

What has been missing from many programs for career advancement is an explicit and transparent connection between career advancement and compensation—the top two drivers of employee retention. These programs, and the technology that can inform employees of their career options, do not typically reflect the compensation impact that the various career options will generate for the employee.

The Plunkett Pay Equity Framework reminds us that transparency about compensation philosophy and practices is extremely important to employees and pay equity. In fact, 77 percent of employees said their employer is not transparent about how people are paid in their organization, according to Salary.com's Pay Equity Pulse Survey.

It is not enough to use a career planning tool to help employees chart their career goals and growth plans through progressive steps and new job titles. Organizations must also reveal the work, training, and skills needed to make that progress and the compensation for doing so.

Similarly, employers deploying the increasingly popular internal talent marketplace must also disclose compensation in these marketplaces. Employees should be able to understand how taking on additional or stretch assignments and acquiring new experience both adds value to the organization and makes a difference in their pay. After all, what marketplace have you ever seen that did not include price/cost/value considerations in the exchange between participants?

Finally, compensation should be a standard element in manager/employee communication about career path and in any performance review. Pay transparency along with career advancement opportunities lead to better communications and fair outcomes.

Working Toward a More Equitable Workplace

One of the aftereffects of the pandemic has been a "Great Re-evaluation" of the role of work in our lives. More than work-life balance, the assessment is fundamental, philosophical, and deeply personal. During the pandemic, "work" often had to be reprioritized, especially when basic needs like health, safety, care for children and elder family members, and sadly even death took precedence. Add to this mix extended periods of increased stress, uncertainty, and conflicting information, And you can see how and why work was suddenly much less important for millions of workers.

The pandemic was not the same for all workers. While many workplaces were shut down completely, others were forced into new modes of working and alternative strategies. Breweries pivoted to making hand sanitizer. Auto manufacturers retooled lines to make personal protective equipment.

And many other workers (grocery store staff, restaurant delivery drivers, meat packing plant workers, etc.) were suddenly deemed "essential." Many of these jobs placed workers in inherently unsafe conditions for extended periods of time. Whether it was the twenty million US workers laid off or furloughed in spring 2020, the millions of office-based workers forced to figure out how to work from home, or the many millions of workers who had to press on with their jobs, we should not have been surprised at the Great Re-evaluation. After all, almost everything changed in 2020–2022. Why would our relationship with work stay the same?

Gen Z and Meaningful Work

While organizations and leaders have been focused on surviving the disruptions caused by the pandemic, other changes have happened in the workplace and to the workforce. One is the emergence of the next generation of workers—Gen Z, which includes people born between 1997 and 2012. According to US Bureau of Labor Statistics data from August 2022, there are over seventeen million workers aged 18–25 in the labor force, accounting for almost 11 percent of the US labor force.[14] And the Gen Z cohort of workers is steadily increasing. Estimates show that by 2030, Gen Z will make up 30 percent of the US workforce.[15, 16]

With a new generation entering the workforce, it's important to understand how they feel about work. When choosing an employer, Gen Z is looking for good work-life balance and learning/development opportunities. In the Deloitte Global 2022 Gen Z & Millennial Survey, nearly 40 percent of Gen Z employees say they have rejected a job or assignment because it did not align with their values. Other important factors are societal and environmental impact of the employer's products and services and a diverse and inclusive culture.[17]

Mental health concerns are particularly important to Gen Z. Nearly half say they feel stressed most or all the time. Forty-six percent feel burned out from the intensity/demands of their working environments. And 44 percent say many people have recently left their organization because of workload pressures.

DEI is also especially important to Gen Z. According to the same Deloitte survey, when Gen Z workers feel that their organization is making progress in creating a diverse and inclusive environment, they are twice as likely to stay than if they feel their organization is not making significant progress in DEI initiatives. Gen Z is much more likely to make career decisions based on alignment with their values. And pay equity will be a value that will factor greatly into these decisions because it concerns both compensation and fundamental fairness.

The Nature of Work Has Changed

The pandemic changed our work and lives in so many ways that it is not possible to count them all. Remote work, shortened hours, and compensation increases to account for difficult and even dangerous conditions are just a few. At the core lies something more basic and fundamental—the role of work in our lives. With years of heightened stress, concerns over family members (especially children and the immunocompromised), rapid disruptions in our workplaces, and ongoing economic concerns, we see work differently now.

Part of this revaluation of work is how individuals wish to invest their working time and energy. It's also tied to core values and how personal values align with organizational values and behaviors.

While each employee's reevaluation is personal, there are at least some common themes we see reflected. The first is the employer's purpose and values. Gen Z and millennials are more willing than prior generations to leave jobs and turn down assignments that don't match their personal values.

LinkedIn data from early 2022 indicate that 80 percent of Gen Z workers who intend to leave their current jobs are seeking a new organization with better alignment to their personal values.[18] As has been said before, and honestly for years, while compensation remains a primary driver of employment decisions, these last few years have complicated the employer-employee relationship and have put noncompensation factors like values and culture at the forefront of HR leaders' agendas.

How Pay Equity Fits into the Reevaluation of Work

Fairness, equity, and inclusion are all part of the values employees want to see reflected in their employers. Standing up for something as fair and fundamental as pay equity enhances an organization's ability to compete for and retain talent.

Yet "organizational culture" has always been challenging to define or measure. We intuitively understand that having a positive, supportive, respectful, and inclusive company culture is desirable. But the connection between culture and organizational performance is hard to assess.

This is where investing in a formal and well-planned pay equity program can make a difference. We can measure the specifics of our pay equity initiatives. The initial analysis, compensation adjustments that are required, and their impact on retention and hiring are measurable and actionable. And the benefits to the organization's culture, while not as directly measurable, will be positive. Pay equity as a fundamental pillar of the organization's values is an essential element of culture, no different from commitments to diversity and inclusion, safety, and the well-being of employees.

The Importance of Skills for Pay Equity

Pay equity is fundamentally about the work. So are skills. When you understand the skills needed to do the work, you can more easily compare different work to get a clearer picture of whether the pay for that work is fair.

But do you know what skills your employees have? Which skills and competencies they need? Do their job descriptions accurately reflect their work and still make sense? Maybe. Maybe not.

Consider the following from Gartner:

- 58 percent of the workforce will need new skill sets to do their jobs successfully.
- Nearly 60 percent of HR leaders reported that building critical skills and competencies was their number one priority in 2022.
- The total number of skills required for a single job has been increasing by 10 percent every year since 2017.
- 47 percent of HR leaders do not know what skill gaps their current employees have.[19]

Turnover costs more than employee retention. Internal recruiting, promotions, development and education, career pathing, and workforce planning all turn the focus away from taking a chance on an external hire to making the most of the HR and talent you already have.

No matter what, you need talent intelligence, foundational data, a skills inventory, newer and better job descriptions and responsibilities, and a way to map it all to each job, each business objective, and each disruption you see coming. So where do you start?

Build a Skills Inventory for Each Employee

What are your employees' talents? What are their personal aspirations? Are you having meaningful career conversations at regular intervals? Are your employees regularly inquiring about job openings or upskilling opportunities? Are you underestimating the capabilities your people have?

But also, are you making greater efforts to hire a diverse workforce and underperforming in how you develop it? Answer those questions and conduct an internal skills and competencies audit. Then organize that data and make your findings part of your business plan so you can scale and operationalize your vision.

Create a Common Skills and Competencies Language and Taxonomy

The next step is creating a common language specific to your industry and your needs based on your market and what's going on in the world around you. This isn't a one-time deal though. It's essential to go through this exercise on a regular basis. It also requires up-to-date and trusted data.

Base job taxonomies and ideal skills and competencies profiles on the structure necessary for growing your company. That will help you understand what your jobs should be and determine the skills and competencies required in each job family.

The Difference between Skills and Competencies

Job skills and job competencies are often confused or conflated. The nuances are important when it comes to structuring your needs for each job. Here's how to look at it:

- Skills are specific abilities you need to perform a job well.
- Competencies are the level of a person's knowledge and behaviors for each skill that is required to be successful in that position.

Competencies are measurable and observable behavior. There are three types of competencies: core competencies, industry competencies, and job family competencies.

Match Skills and Competencies to the Job

The proficiency level of a competency lets you know the level of expertise a candidate or employee must possess in that skill to perform a job to the highest degree of excellence.

Now take your new job taxonomies, your skills inventory, what you know about your future goals, and what you know about the growth opportunities your employees are looking for and sort the data.

The tricky part is doing the initial talent intelligence legwork, and we don't recommend doing it alone. Since you now have uniform, taxonomized job classifications and descriptions, and you've prioritized your needs, AI can do a big chunk of the rest, including helping you identify the right employees for the right jobs.

Think of it as computer matchmaking, but for jobs. Instead of "loves long walks on the beach and reading poetry," it can be "proficient in coding in JavaScript, HTML, Python, CSS" or "has a mixed background in engineering, technical writing, and sales, and excellent written and verbal communications soft skills." It might be time for a blind date with a sales engineering job or customer success role.

Personalized Learning Is the Key to Developing Skills and Competencies

The next step is how you "coach them up," as they say in sports. How do you upskill, train, and develop employees and apply their talents in different capacity? That largely depends on the person's complete skills and competencies profile, their personality, their personal goals, and all the unique things about that person's makeup.

HR business partners and team managers can survey employees and follow up one on one to understand how to tailor personalized plans to each employee, or possibly to each group of similar employees. Map out their employee journeys, find the necessary classes or trainings they need, continuously engage that employee, and keep them on the path that works for both of you.

It's not a good journey unless it's one you can take together. Again, remember that the cost of a class or the time and effort it takes to actively develop an employee is nothing compared to the cost of hiring a new one.

Upskilling and Reskilling Are the Best Ways to Close Capability Gaps

When asked to prioritize reskilling existing employees, shifting current employees to new roles, recruiting, and hiring new talent from other firms, or contracting out jobs, executives overwhelmingly said that building skills with their current teams was the best way to close their organization's skills gaps.

Whether you're in banking and financial services, construction, education, energy, software, manufacturing, healthcare, hospitality, retail, pharmaceutical, or media and publishing, it's clear that focusing on skills and competencies is essential. There's a solution for companies that have poor internal mobility, that have high voluntary turnover, and that struggle to find top talent with the right skills.

The answer is moving to personalized, skills-based learning and a skill-centric approach to talent management. This change requires HR shifting its role to a data-driven strategic adviser and partner across your organization.

Organizations can start by structuring talent management around talent intelligence and building a skills and competencies framework to create a blueprint for growth through hiring, recruiting, retention, talent assessment, and learning and development. Here's what you'll need:

- **Talent Intelligence**: A skills and competency data framework and cloud management tool for HR, compensation, organizational development, talent management, and recruiting.
- **Enterprise HR Systems**: System-agnostic HR software that can seamlessly connect with enterprise resource planning (ERP) platforms (such as Workday, Oracle, and SAP) and help you craft the precise job descriptions and determine the exact skill sets you need at every level, offer competitive salaries and benefits, achieve pay equity, and have specifically tailored compensation analysis and market data at the click of a button.
- **Scalable and Future-Proof Processes**: Not only do you need buy-in from executives at the highest levels to transition into a skills-based organization, you need seasoned professionals with compensation, HR, and data science expertise to help you continuously update and manage your skills-based HR practices.

Feeding talent intelligence into your performance management and foundational tools will get you pretty far, but you need a way to take all of the outside data possible and every piece of internal information from your own skills inventory and then plot your path forward. By empowering employees to pursue their own advancement with the same company, having pay transparency, better communication, and being open and honest about the path forward—upskilling becomes the ultimate win-win.

Twelve Reasons You May Need a Skills and Competencies Framework

1. **Difficulty Recruiting and Hiring the Right People**: If a company is having difficulty finding qualified candidates for open positions, a skills and competencies framework can help them identify the specific skills and competencies that are required for those roles. This can make it easier to attract and hire the right people and can also help reduce the time and cost of hiring.

2. **Poor Performance Management**: If a company is not effectively managing employee performance, a skills and competencies framework can help them define the specific behaviors that are expected of employees in different roles. This can make it easier to provide meaningful feedback and coaching and can also help improve employee performance.

3. **Ineffective Training and Development**: If a company is not effectively training and developing their employees, a skills and competencies framework can help them identify the specific skills and knowledge that their employees need to be successful. This can help improve employee skills and knowledge, which can lead to improved employee performance and productivity.

4. **Unclear Career Paths**: If a company does not have clear career paths for their employees, then employees may be less motivated to stay with the company and develop their skills. A skills and competencies framework can help create clear career paths for employees, which can motivate them to stay with the company and develop their skills.

5. **High Employee Turnover**: If a company has high employee turnover, it can be costly and disruptive. A skills and competencies framework can help reduce employee turnover by providing employees with opportunities to develop their skills and knowledge, which can make them more satisfied with their jobs.

6. **Lack of Diversity and Inclusion**: If a company does not have a diverse and inclusive workforce, it may be missing out on new ideas and perspectives. A skills and competencies framework can help identify and address any gaps in diversity and inclusion, which can lead to a more innovative and productive workforce.

7. **Not Meeting Business Goals**: If a company is not meeting its business goals, it may be due to a lack of the right skills and competencies. A skills and competencies framework can help identify the skills and competencies that are needed to meet the company's goals and can then be used to develop and implement training and development programs to help employees acquire those skills and competencies.

8. **Compliance Issues**: If a company is subject to industry regulations, it may be required to have employees with certain skills and competencies. A skills and competencies framework can help identify the skills and competencies that are required to meet regulatory requirements and can then be used to develop and implement training and development programs to help employees acquire those skills and competencies.

9. **Organizational Change**: If a company is undergoing a major organizational change, such as a merger or acquisition, a skills and competencies framework can help identify the skills and competencies that are needed to successfully implement the change.

10. **Lack of Alignment between Business Goals and Employee Skills**: If there is a mismatch between the skills that employees have and the skills that are needed to achieve the company's goals, this can lead to a number of problems, including low productivity, poor customer service, and missed opportunities. A skills and competencies framework can help identify and address this misalignment.

11. **Inability to Measure Employee Performance**: If a company is not able to measure employee performance against the skills and competencies that are required for the role, it is difficult to identify which employees are performing well and which employees need additional development. A skills and competencies framework can help provide a framework for measuring employee performance.

12. **Lack of Transparency and Fairness in Employee Rewards**: If employees do not understand how their performance is evaluated and how their rewards are determined, this can lead to dissatisfaction and a lack of motivation. A skills and competencies framework can help make the employee evaluation and rewards process more transparent and fair.

Making a Positive Impact through Pay Equity

by Steve Boese

The philosophy behind the Plunkett Pay Equity Framework is that pay serves as the quantitative measure of an employee's value and the heart of the deal between employees and employers. It's a natural focal point when a company asks, "Are we treating our people fairly?"

If pay is the heart of the agreement between the employee and the employer, then a responsible organization must ensure that pay is administered and delivered to employees equitably. The Plunkett Pay Equity Framework defines pay equity as "equal pay for comparable jobs that is internally equitable, externally competitive, and transparently communicated."

Like many important organizational goals, achieving pay equity sounds relatively simple. At a basic level, reaching agreement and buy-in on treating people fairly is not difficult. After all, what CEO or HR leader would disagree with fair pay for all employees?

But like many other seemingly simple ideas, pay equity has, for many years and for many reasons, been difficult for most organizations to reach. It doesn't have to be that way.

For organizations open to taking their first steps towards equitable pay and to making the needed changes to systems, processes, and antiquated ways of thinking about compensation, both the Plunkett Pay Equity Framework and the information and recommendations in this book provide ample resources, research, and justification to begin your organization's journey.

Everyone Benefits from Pay Equity

Who benefits from a commitment to the development of equitable pay? In short, everyone. Let's break down the impacts of achieving pay equity on the various groups of stakeholders of the organization.

Employees. For employees, the benefits of pay equity are the clearest and most immediate. The employee-level effects of an ongoing commitment to pay equity are all positive. For many employees in a typical organization, they will see an increase in their base compensation and/or additional payments designed to correct for historical pay gaps.

For example, the software company Salesforce, who has famously adopted pay fairness as a pillar of their corporate culture since 2015, reported that ongoing compensation analysis led to pay adjustments for 8.5 percent of their global employees between 2015 and 2022.[20] In total, Salesforce has allocated $22 million in additional employee compensation, calculated from seven annual review cycles, to correct historical pay inequities in their compensation practices. So, at the outset, conducting the processes of review and analysis of compensation will likely lead to compensation increases, particularly for those employees who have been traditionally undercompensated for a variety of reasons, including gender, ethnicity, and age.

Employees see additional benefits of pay equity that go beyond personal, direct compensation. We have seen numerous employee surveys on the reasons people join and stay or leave organizations. Fairness, contributing positively and responsibly in the community, and organizational alignment with an employee's personal values are all important factors to employees today.

A commitment to pay equity is one of the few HR-related programs and interventions that address almost all issues employees care most about—compensation, fairness, purpose, community reputation, and values aligned with their own. Employees see pay equity as one of the strongest benefits the organization can provide, which helps strengthen their commitment to the organization, their colleagues, and their career decisions.

Human Resources. HR resides in that tricky intersection between organizational goals and constraints, and employees' needs and aspirations. Making the difficult decisions that effectively balance these sometimes-competing motivations stands at the heart of HR. But designing and implementing a pay equity program throughout the organization is one of the times when an "HR" program well serves both sets of competing goals.

When pay equity is effectively communicated, carefully implemented, and ingrained in the organization's processes and culture, it can transform both the function of HR and the perception of HR throughout the organization. All HR professionals should desire to make progress in pay equity—if not for the clear benefits for employees and the organization, then for how it will impact their own careers and the function of HR. Delivering on such an important and strategic initiative is the highest aspiration for HR leaders and teams and something they can be extremely proud of undertaking.

Organization. Very few founders and entrepreneurs set out to create a business that ends up treating employees unfairly. Go read as many "About Us" pages on company websites as you can stand. You won't find "unfairness" stated in any of the founding stories, mission statements, and list of company values.

No leader sets out to build and run an organization that ends up with unfairness, bias, lack of transparency, and entrenched cynicism around compensation policies. But in many, if not most organizations, some or all these factors emerge in compensation programs and how employees are treated overall. But over time and with organizational growth it "just happens." Realizing the problem is the first step to addressing it.

Community. The compensation data for underrepresented and disadvantaged groups struggling with pay inequity issues are profound and reveal systemic issues impacting individuals and the greater community. Pay equity problems in the US, particularly, have been endemic in society and perpetuated by traditional compensation practices for decades. Persistent salary and wage gaps permeate the US and other advanced economies, leading to widespread threats to economic stability and individual financial security.

Ongoing pay inequities combined with lack of progress towards true pay equity in the workplace means that many women, people of color, disabled workers, and others are perpetually underpaid, and often underemployed. These losses accumulate and grow over time.

As a result, many of these workers are less able to build savings, withstand economic downturns, and achieve some measure of economic stability. The US census data released in September 2022 confirmed that the harshest effects of the gender wage gap continue to fall on women of color, with many of them experiencing the largest gender pay gaps among all workers. While there are many who call for intervention by federal, state, and even local governments to pursue measures that strengthen equal pay protections, reduce workplace bias, and promote fairness and equity, employers have the most important part to play in driving pay equity for all. If ever achieved, along with progress on diversity in leadership, this would reduce economic inequality and secure greater economic stability for all.

While elements of working towards pay equity can sometimes feel extremely complex, abstract, and a bit scary (like "multivariate regression analysis"), the core of the issue is very human. It lies in our responses to questions like

- What does our organization stand for?
- How do we treat our colleagues?
- What values should the organizations in our community and society reflect? (and importantly)
- What kind of world of work do we want for our children?

Recommendations

Like any operational transformation, adopting pay equity requires sincere commitment at all levels of the organization. This commitment must begin with the most senior leadership in the organization including the CEO. Because adopting pay equity requires investments in time, resources, and money and can affect the bottom line, the highest level of commitment is needed to ensure that the initiatives take hold and make a difference.

Important roles like executive sponsor and project owner/manager should be designated and assigned at the very start of the project. Ideally, the project manager will be dedicated to the project full-time, at least for one full cycle of data gathering, analysis, and implementation of compensation. Additional resources, subject matter experts, and lawyers will be needed to effectively audit, monitor, maintain, and address pay equity. Every effort should be made to support the project team. Nothing says "this project is not really that important" to the greater organization more than not dedicating the right people and resources to the effort.

Communication is also essential. The communications owner should be a key leader in the project team and experienced in the structure, preferred methods of communication, and culture of the organization. Communication should be frequent, transparent, and repetitive—there is so much information overload in the workplace that many messages take time to register with a busy workforce. Pay equity communications should include the following:

- This is what we are doing.
- Here is why we are doing this.
- Here is the process.
- Here is what we expect to happen.
- This is how you may be impacted.
- Here is how we will measure results and make changes.

One of the goals of a commitment to pay equity is to become an organization known for that commitment. Comprehensive and frequent communication is one way to build that positive reputation.

Training people about pay equity and compensation in general is also important and can be an extension of the communication process. Everyone involved in compensation-related decisions should understand the organization's compensation philosophy, strategy, and policies and that pay equity is essential to all of them.

Each organization will have a unique path to pay equity. Open and transparent communication includes sharing the important data points and progress made as well as areas where perhaps the progress has been slow or fallen short.

Here, comparisons can be made to commitments to achieve specific goals in representation as a part of their DEI initiatives. These organizations periodically publish both the goals and the progress against them. Quite often, they have then had to explain why actual progress has fallen short of their goals. The ones with the best approach are open and transparent about what they have learned and what they are doing to address their shortcomings. While these reports can be hard to publish for the organization, they reinforce the commitment of leadership and demonstrate accountability— both important to keep the energy and momentum of the program moving forward.

This same commitment to sharing pay equity goals, reporting progress against the goals (even if only for internal use), and documenting actions taken to improve progress must be a regular and fundamental component of the pay equity initiative.

Conclusion

We are dealing with a labor shortage and an increasingly diverse working population. The reality is, we need everybody. A commitment to pay equity and DEI is crucial to the successful organization of the future. Organizations who both survive and thrive will be the ones who are committed to the values, actions, and outcomes for pay equity.

Endnotes

1. What Is Pay Equity?

1. "California Equal Pay Act: Frequently Asked Questions," California Department of Industrial Relations, updated June 2023, https://www.dir.ca.gov/dlse/california_equal_pay_act.htm

2. New York Labor Law Chapter 31, Article 6, Section 190, "Definitions," The New York State Senate, 2014, https://www.nysenate.gov/legislation/laws/LAB/190

3. New York Labor Law Chapter 31, Article 6, Section 198-C, "Benefits or Wage Supplements," The New York State Senate, 2014, https://www.nysenate.gov/legislation/laws/LAB/198-C

4. "Equal Pay for Equal Work Law; Definitions," Minnesota Statutes Section 181.66, 2022, https://www.revisor.mn.gov/statutes/cite/181.66

2. The Gender Pay Gap

1. "The Gender Pay Gap," American Association of University Women, 2020, https://www.aauw.org/issues/equity/pay-gap/; "The Simple Truth About the Gender Pay Gap," American Association of University Women, 2020, https://www.aauw.org/resources/research/simple-truth/; "Deeper in Debt: Women and Student Loans," American Association of University Women, 2020, https://www.aauw.org/resources/research/deeper-in-debt/

2. Valentin Bolotnyy and Natalia Emanuel, "How Unpredictable Schedules Widen the Gender Pay Gap," Harvard Business Review, July 1, 2022, https://hbr.org/2022/07/how-unpredictable-schedules-widen-the-gender-pay-gap

3. Alexis Krivkovich, et al., "Women in the Workplace", McKinsey & Company, October 18, 2022, https://www.mckinsey.com/~/media/mckinsey/featured%20insights/diversity%20and%20inclusion/women%20in%20the%20workplace%202022/women-in-the-workplace-2022.pdf

4. Krivkovich, "Women in the Workplace."

5. Karen Offen, "The Male Breadwinner Model: How a 19th Century Theory Limits Women's Economic Opportunities," Economica: Women and the Global Economy,

International Museum of Women, 2023, https://exhibitions.globalfundforwomen.org/economica/property-and-wealth/male-breadwinner-model

6. Jone Johnson Lewis, "A Short History of Women's Property Rights in the United States," ThoughtCo., updated July 13, 2019, https://www.thoughtco.com/property-rights-of-women-3529578

7. Melissa Block, "Yes, Women Could Vote After the 19th Amendment—But Not All Women. Or Men," NPR Morning Edition, August 26, 2020, https://www.npr.org/2020/08/26/904730251/yes-women-could-vote-after-the-19th-amendment-but-not-all-women-or-men

8. Jessica Hill, "Fact Check: Post Detailing 9 Things Women Couldn't Do before 1971 Is Mostly Right," USA Today, October 28, 2020, https://www.usatoday.com/story/news/factcheck/2020/10/28/fact-check-9-things-women-couldnt-do-1971-mostly-right/3677101001/

9. *Meritor Savings Bank v. Vinson*, 477 US 57 (1986).

10. Megan Brenan, "Women Still Handle Main Household Tasks in US," Gallup, January 29, 2020, https://news.gallup.com/poll/283979/women-handle-main-household-tasks.aspx

11. Sarah Jane Glynn, "Breadwinning Mothers Are Critical to Families' Economic Security," Center for American Progress, March 29, 2021, https://www.americanprogress.org/article/breadwinning-mothers-critical-familys-economic-security/

12. Emma Hinchliffe, "The Female CEOs on This Year's Fortune 500 Just Broke Three All-Time Records," Fortune, June 2, 2021, https://fortune.com/2021/06/02/female-ceos-fortune-500-2021-women-ceo-list-roz-brewer-walgreens-karen-lynch-cvs-thasunda-brown-duckett-tiaa/

13. "Employment and Earnings by Occupation," US Department of Labor's Women's Bureau, 2021, https://www.dol.gov/agencies/wb/data/occupations

14. Robin Bleiweis, "Quick Facts About the Gender Wage Gap," Center for American Progress, March 24, 2020, https://www.americanprogress.org/article/quick-facts-gender-wage-gap/

15. Elise Gould, "Black–White Wage Gaps Are Worse Today Than in 2000," Economic Policy Institute: Working Economics Blog, February 27, 2020, https://www.epi.org/blog/Black-white-wage-gaps-are-worse-today-than-in-2000/

16. Gould, "Black–White Wage Gaps."

17. Claire Cain Miller, Kevin Quealy, and Margot Sanger-Katz, "The Top Jobs Where Women Are Outnumbered by Men Named John," New York Times, April 24, 2018, https://www.nytimes.com/interactive/2018/04/24/upshot/women-and-men-named-john.html

4. Pay Equity as Part of a Larger Compensation Strategy

1. "Employment Cost Index," US Bureau of Labor Statistics, March 2023, https://www.bls.gov/eci/home.htm

2. Candice Wolken, "Creating a Compensation Philosophy," Salary.com, March 5, 2019, https://www.salary.com/blog/creating-a-compensation-philosophy/#sample-compensation-philosophy

3. Staff at Salary.com, "The Importance of Pay Philosophies," Salary.com, May 1, 2018, https://www.salary.com/blog/the-importance-of-pay-philosophies/

6. Pay Gaps and Discrimination

1. Tyler Vigen, "Spurious Correlations," https://www.tylervigen.com/spurious-correlations

7. Managing Wage Compression and Pay Equity

1. Molly Lipson, "No More Fridays: A Real-World Experiment Just Proved That We Should All Shift to a Four-day Workweek," Business Insider, January 17, 2023, https://www.businessinsider.com/4-day-workweek-successful-trial-evidence-productivity-retention-revenue-2023-1

8. The Labor Shortage

1. Mark Foulon, et al., "The War for Talent," McKinsey Quarterly, January 1998, https://www.researchgate.net/profile/Mark-Foulon-2/publication/284689712_The_War_for_Talent/links/58d103b94585158476f366f6/The-War-for-Talent.pdf; Charles Fishman, "The War for Talent," Fast Company, July 31, 1998, https://www.fastcompany.com/34512/war-talent

2. "War for Talent," Google Trends, 2004 to present, https://trends.google.com/trends/explore?date=all&geo=US&q=%22war%20for%20talent%22

3. "Labor Shortage," Google Trends, 2004 to present, https://trends.google.com/trends/explore?date=all&geo=US&q=%22labor%20shortage%22

4. "US Fertility Rate 1950–2023," Macrotrends, https://www.macrotrends.net/countries/USA/united-states/fertility-rate

5. "US Unemployment Rate 1948–2023," Data Commons Timelines, https://datacommons.org/tools/timeline#&place=country/USA&statsVar=UnemploymentRate_Person

6. "American Community Survey, S0502: Selected Characteristics of the Foreign-Born Population by Period of Entry into the United States," US Census Bureau, https://data.census.gov/table?q=United+States&g=0100000US&tid=ACSST1Y2021.S0502

7. "Immigrant Share of the US Population and Civilian Labor Force, 1980–Present," Migration Policy Institute, https://www.migrationpolicy.org/programs/data-hub/charts/immigrant-share-us-population-and-civilian-labor-force

8. "Understanding America's Labor Shortage," US Chamber of Commerce, October 2022, https://www.uschamber.com/workforce/understanding-americas-labor-shortage

9. "Understanding America's Labor Shortage."

10. Abha Bhattarai, "Worker Shortages Are Fueling America's Biggest Labor Crises," The Washington Post, September 16, 2022, https://www.washingtonpost.com/business/2022/09/16/worker-shortage-strikes-economy/

11. Ashley Abramson, "Burnout and Stress Are Everywhere," American Psychological Association 2022 Trends Report, January 1, 2022, https://www.apa.org/monitor/2022/01/special-burnout-stress

12. Sue Cantrell, et al., "Building Tomorrow's Skills-Based Organization: Jobs Aren't Working Anymore," Deloitte, 2022, https://www2.deloitte.com/content/dam/Deloitte/global/Documents/Deloitte-Skills-Based-Organization.pdf

13. PKim Parker and Juliana Menasce Horowitz, "Majority of Workers Who Quit a Job in 2021 Cite Low Pay, No Opportunities for Advancement, Feeling Disrespected," Pew Research Center, March 9, 2022, https://www.pewresearch.org/shortreads/2022/03/09/majority-of-workers-who-quit-a-job-in-2021-cite-low-pay-no-opportunities-for-advancement-feeling-disrespected/

14. "Table A-9. Selected Employment Indicators, 1948–2023," Economic Research, FRED Economic Data, US Bureau of Labor Statistics, https://fred.stlouisfed.org/release/tables?rid=50&eid=2698#snid=2705

15. KVibha Sathesh Kumar, "Gen Z in the Workplace: How Should Companies Adapt?," Johns Hopkins University, April 18, 2023, https://imagine.jhu.edu/blog/2023/04/18/gen-z-in-the-workplace-how-should-companies-adapt

16. Chloe Berger, "Gen Z Workers Will Be 30% of the Workforce by 2030—Here's What They Want from Their Employers," Yahoo Finance, May 27, 2022, https://finance.yahoo.com/news/gen-z-workers-30-workforce-123000932.html?guccounter=1&guce_referrer=aHR0cHM6Ly93d3cuZ29vZ2xlLmNvbS8&guce_referrer_sig=AQAAAFonoOtEgtO-dJeO6dhL1IukMWhZ8rY4dB2sPP6WbngP0E1F3aLBv5AK5hCXPBfuqF71ki-bFUZBh_a6eH6FVI248_9oja3FytOLaA7ZomnOLUe3oIUEq-RVqJqCc7QhHxo_HHpIAgQuqWr-drKFn6zQ63s2w1LcsKlnFcfM0Esh

17. "Striving for Balance, Advocating for Change: The Deloitte Global 2022 Gen Z & Millennial Survey," Deloitte, 2022, https://www2.deloitte.com/content/dam/ insights/articles/glob175227_global-millennial-and-gen-z-survey/Gen%20Z%20 and%20Millennial%20Survey%202022_Final.pdf

18. George Anders, "Is Gen Z the Boldest Generation? Its Job-Hunt Priorities Are Off the Charts," LinkedIn News, February 9, 2022, https://www.linkedin.com/pulse/ genz-boldest-generation-its-job-hunt-priorities-off-charts-anders/?trackingId= pwWrCQQ1SiG9Yds3hH8gUg%3D%3D

19. Mary Baker and Teresa Zuech, "Gartner HR Research Finds 58% of the Workforce Will Need New Skill Sets to Do Their Jobs Successfully," Gartner, February 4, 2021, https://www.gartner.com/en/newsroom/press-releases/2021-02-03-gartner-hr- research-finds-fifty-eight-percent-of-the-workforce-will-need-new-skill-sets-to-do- their-jobs-successfully

20. Brent Hyder, "2022 Equal Pay Update: The Salesforce Approach to Pay Fairness," Salesforce News & Insights, March 30, 2022, https://www.salesforce.com/news/ stories/2022-equal-pay-update-the-salesforce-approach-to-pay-fairness/

Index

About the Authors

Steve Boese

Steve Boese is one of the cofounders of H3 HR Advisors, a leading HR technology advisory and services consultancy. Since 2013, Steve has been the program chair and host of the HR Technology Conference, the world's largest gathering of the global HR technology community, and authors a monthly HR Technology Column for *Human Resource Executive* magazine. He is a frequent speaker and author on topics in human resources, HR technology, and the world of work. Steve created and has cohosted since 2009 the *HR Happy Hour* show and podcast, the longest-running and most downloaded podcast in the human resources field. Additionally, he cohosts the *At Work in America* podcast and the first human resources podcast tailored for Amazon Alexa-enabled devices, *The Workplace Minute* powered by H3 HR Advisors. Steve has spoken at numerous events in human resources and HR technology all over the world, including events in Barcelona, Singapore, and Shanghai.

Heather Bussing

Heather Bussing is a California employment attorney, writer, and law professor. Her focus is providing sensible and strategic advice to employers. Heather's experience with business, humans, technology, and work gives her a unique perspective focused on preventing and solving problems rather than fighting about them.

Heather is a contributing editor to HRExaminer and regularly speaks, writes, and edits for HR technology.

Heather has been interviewed and quoted in the New York Times, Wall Street Journal, CNN, Business Insider, and NPR. She writes a daily column for Salary.com's Compensation and Pay Equity Newsletter on the latest in employment laws, covering pay equity and transparency, AI in HR Tech, and why compliance, diversity, and fairness are good business.

George LaRocque

George LaRocque, founder of WorkTech, has more than twenty-five years in the human capital management (HCM) industry. A former practitioner in talent acquisition, talent management, and HR, he turned technology vendor executive for some of the market's largest brands. Now he's an HCM market analyst and advisor focused on users and developers of HR technology. He was the publisher and founder of HRWins research and reports on workforce trends and related innovation in tech. He was instrumental in launching the UNLEASH media business and site during 2020. He helps employers understand the trends that are impacting their workforce today and in the future. He helps HR service providers and technology vendors with a unique perspective on HR customers and the changing workforce.

Madeline Laurano

Madeline Laurano is the founder and chief analyst of Aptitude Research. For over eighteen years, Madeline's primary focus has been on the human capital management (HCM) market, specializing in talent acquisition and employee experience. Her work helps companies both validate and re-evaluate their strategies and understand the role technology can play in driving business outcomes. She has watched HCM transform from a back-office function to a strategic company initiative with a focus on partnerships, experience, and efficiency.

Before founding Aptitude Research, Madeline held research roles at Aberdeen, Bersin by Deloitte, ERE Media, and Brandon Hall Group. She is the coauthor of *Best Practices in Leading a Global Workforce* and is often quoted in leading business publications including the *Wall Street Journal*, the

Boston Globe, Yahoo News, the *New York Times*, and the *Financial Times*. She is a frequent presenter at industry conferences including the HR Technology Conference and Exposition, SHRM, IHRIM, HCI's Strategic Talent Acquisition conference, Unleash, GDS International's HCM Summit, and HRO Today.

Sarah Morgan

Sarah Morgan (she/her) is a recovering HR executive turned DEI leader. She is currently the director of equity and inclusion for Humareso, where she provides consulting and coaching surrounding inclusive and equitable organizational culture and practical, people-centric leadership. Under Sarah's leadership, Humareso was named one of the Top 15 DEI Companies to Work With in 2023.

Sarah now keynotes conferences and has been featured in major publications, including the CUE Labor Relations conference, SHRM, *Forge* by Medium, *Fast Company*, *Essence*, CNN, and *Black Enterprise Magazine*. She also serves on the board of advisors for the UKG Workforce Institute and the board of directors at Marbles Kids Museum. She is the creator and host of the *Leading in Color* podcast, a show centering on cultivating positive workplace experiences through diversity, inclusion, and social consciousness. She also hosts the *Inclusion Crusade* on the HR Happy Hour network.

Sarah has been named to *HR Executive Magazine*'s Top 100 HR Influencers, Clear Company's 50 Unstoppable Women in HR Tech, and the XpertHR UK List of Top Global HR Voices. Her blog was named to Proven's Best HR Blogs, BambooHR's Top HR Blogs, PayScale's 25 Must-Read HR Blogs, and Wonolo's 50 Best Blogs for HR Pros for consecutive years.

She holds a bachelor's degree in communication studies with a focus on organizational communication and leadership from the University of Richmond as well as a master's degree in human resources management.

When not working, Sarah is a wife and mom with a blended family of five children living outside Durham, NC. She enjoys mindlessly binging reality television, spending time with friends and family, reading, scrolling, eating, and long naps with her dog.

Kent Plunkett

Kent Plunkett is the CEO and founder of Salary.com. Kent is as passionate about compensation and pay equity as he was in 1999 when he co-founded Salary.com with a goal of reinventing how employers and employees access compensation data.

Kent has always believed pay equity is a two-sided coin and designed the business to support that belief. The company's groundbreaking Salary Wizard was the first tool employees could access to understand their worth, effectively lifting the veil on salary information for millions of employees annually. On the B2B side, Salary.com has become the preeminent provider of compensation market data, software, and analytics, serving over 30,000 survey participant organizations, 8,000 business-to-business software subscribers, and 45+ million employees globally.

Kent holds an MBA from Harvard Business School and A.B. in Economics and Government from Georgetown University. He is a three-time Inc. 500 CEO, a six-time Deloitte Fast 50 awardee and recipient of the 2007 Ernst & Young Entrepreneur of Year Award for business services. Kent is accredited by WorldatWork as a Certified Compensation Professional (CCP®)

Trish Steed

Trish Steed is the cofounder of H3 HR Advisors, a leading HR technology advisory and services consultancy. Trish cohosts the *HR Happy Hour* podcast and the *At Work in America* podcast on the HR Happy Hour Network. She also created the HR Happy Hour *WORK BREAK!* vlog.

A former HR executive and human capital management (HCM) product leader with over twenty years of experience in Big 4 public accounting, PR, healthcare, manufacturing, and IT, Trish brings that knowledge to her clients as an analyst and advisor. She is a frequent speaker at global HR and other business events including acting as the chairwoman of HR Tech China in Shanghai; keynoting the HR Summit in Dubai; and speaking at events in Singapore, London, and Paris. Trish graduated from Webster University with an MA in Human Resource Management and also holds a BA in Sociology and a minor in Political Science from the University of Missouri. She's a working mother who loves writing, painting, and volunteering for organizations that help children.

John Sumser

John Sumser is a vice-president of marketing at Salary.com where he uses his decades of experience as an independent analyst covering HR technology and its impact on people and work.

Sumser's work includes deep research into HR technology to identify and explain rapidly evolving trends. Built on a foundation of engineering, design, and philosophy, John seeks to understand where technology works best, for whom, and in what context. John has been actively involved with Salary.com and its products from start-up to its initial public offering (IPO) as a director, and since Kent Plunkett and investors' reacquisition of the company.

Colophon

by Heather Bussing

Pay equity is hard to understand and even harder to do. Creating a book about pay equity is also challenging. This book exists because of the creativity, talents, and painstaking work of many people behind the scenes. Everything—fonts, colors, graphics, page layout, cover, and even the index—required exploring ideas, trying things, disagreements, revisions, and difficult choices. It's like building a home for words and ideas.

Here is more information on how and why this book looks the way it does and who helped make it.

Graphics by Jen Demore, Caitlin Schiattareggia, Bambi Xiao, and Stela Yordanova of Salary.com.

Interior and ebook by Robert Kern (interior design), Alice White (copy editing), Joey Lien (composition), Olivia Turner (proofreading), and Patrick Hunter (indexing) of TIPS Publishing Services, Carrboro, NC. TIPS composed the book using Segoe and Bembo fonts in InDesign.

Cover by Jeff Puda Book Design.

Printing by Gasch Printing using a Canon 3900 ColorStream Inkjet continuous feed press and binding with a Horizon BQ470 inline binder.

SHRM's book publishing team: Matt Davis, Montrese Hamilton, and Ashley Miller.

Music we enjoyed while working included WCPE (The Classic Station), *Respect* by Aretha Franklin, *Run the World* by Beyoncé, *Stronger* by Kelly Clarkson, and *Juice* by Lizzo.

Snacks that sustained us included Thin Mints, string cheese, and Diet Coke.

Dog walks were innumerable!